GORY & GRUESOME HISTORY

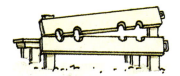

CONTENTS

Guilty!	2
Disaster!	33
Sick!	65
Dead!	97
Index	128

W
FRANKLIN WATTS
NEW YORK • LONDON • SYDNEY

LAW AND ORDER

Laws have been written down for at least 4,000 years. The oldest that we know of were written by the Sumerian king, Ur-Nammu, about 2100 BC.

Hammurabi, the king of Babylon from 1792 to 1750 BC, later set down more detailed laws. The Greeks, Jews and Romans added to and improved these laws. Most of our modern laws are based on Roman law or on Anglo-Saxon law.

The Ten Commandments given to Moses by God about 3,000 years ago were laws which told the Jews how they should behave.

The Ten Commandments
Worship no god but me.
Do not make for yourselves images.
Do not use my name for evil purposes.
Observe the Sabbath and keep it holy.
Respect your father and your mother.
Do not commit murder.
Do not commit adultery.
Do not steal.
Do not accuse anyone falsely.
Do not desire another man's house; do not desire his wife, his slaves, his cattle, his donkeys, or anything else that he owns.

In Saxon times, someone who killed another person had to pay a sum of money, called *wergild* (blood money) to the family of his victim.

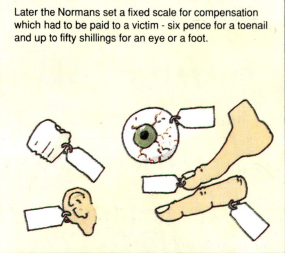

Later the Normans set a fixed scale for compensation which had to be paid to a victim - six pence for a toenail and up to fifty shillings for an eye or a foot.

In ancient China, if somebody accused of a crime was found to be innocent, the accuser was punished instead.

Animals can also be subject to laws. In AD 864, a church court in Germany 'executed' a hive of bees which had stung a man to death.

The law code of the Babylonian King Hammurabi was very severe. If a son hit his father, the son's hand could be chopped off.

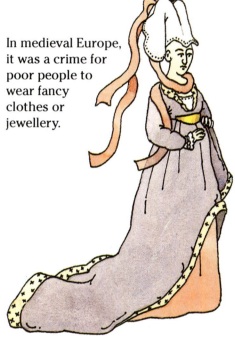

In medieval Europe, it was a crime for poor people to wear fancy clothes or jewellery.

The original Hooligans were a family of Irish immigrants who lived in London in the nineteenth century. They were renowned for their violence and lawlessness.

Solon the Law-giver gave a new system of law which was gentler than the previous system to the Greeks of Athens in the sixth century BC.

Solon the Law-giver

International law

The Romans introduced a system of laws called the *Jus Feciale* for all the countries in their Empire. Roman law is the basis for much modern law, including international law.

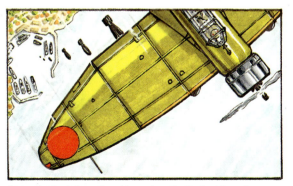

Japan broke international law when it attacked American ships in Pearl Harbor, Hawaii, in 1941, without declaring war. If Japan had declared war on America beforehand, it would have been behaving quite legally.

It was once thought that if a baby's fingernails were cut before its first birthday, it would turn out to be a thief.

STOP THIEF!

Theft is the most common of all crimes and laws against it date back at least 4,000 years. Professional thieves have often formed themselves into gangs. The 'Wild Bunch', led by Butch Cassidy and the Sundance Kid, was a small gang which terrorised the Western Frontier from South Dakota to New Mexico. Some gangs, such as the Mafia, have grown into huge criminal organisations, which profit from many different types of crime.

The last American stagecoach robbery was in 1899. It was carried out by a woman called Pearl Hart.

Billy the Kid (William Bonney 1859-1881) was said to have shot 21 men in the Wild West. He was first jailed for stealing clothes from a Chinese laundry in 1875.

Jesse James once lent a poor widow $800 to repay her debt to a bank. He then robbed the bank and took his money back.

Rogues' Gallery

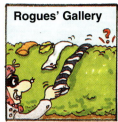    

A bawdy basket was a woman who stole clothes drying on garden hedges.

Anglers stole valuables from open windows using hooks on poles.

Diving belles were female pickpockets in Tudor England.

Footpads stalked their prey on foot. They were muggers.

Highwaymen rode horses and stole from travellers.

When Ned Kelly, the Australian outlaw, was captured in Glenrowan, Australia, in 1880, he was wearing a suit of bullet-proof armour made from melted-down and reshaped ploughshares.

The famous 'Wild Bunch'. Butch Cassidy is seated on the right, and the Sundance Kid is on the left.

The pirate captain Bluebeard used to hang lighted wicks beneath his hat to make himself look frightening.

Organised crime

The Mafia is a network of Sicilian criminal organizations. During the 1890s, Sicilian immigrants introduced it into the USA.

The Japanese Yakuza wear tattoos and execute their victims with swords.

The Triads are Chinese criminal gangs. They prey on Chinese communities throughout the world.

FRAUD AND FORGERY

Some criminals use lies or trickery to steal money or gain power. Forgers manufacture false documents or works of art, which they pass off as genuine. Computer fraud may be carried out by giving false information to computers.

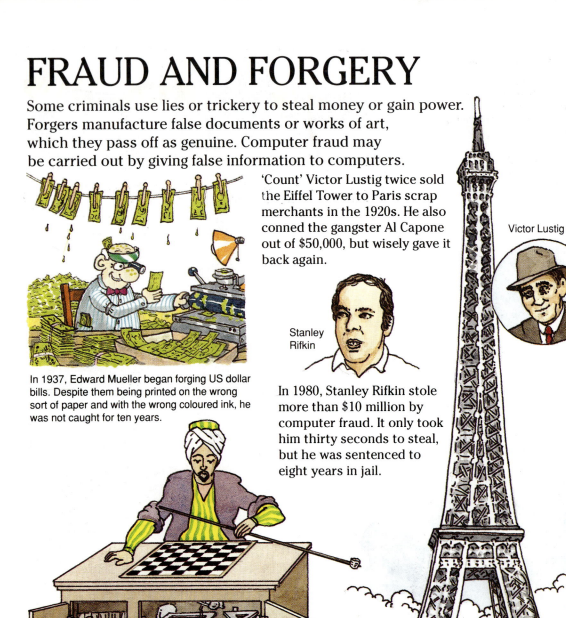

'Count' Victor Lustig twice sold the Eiffel Tower to Paris scrap merchants in the 1920s. He also conned the gangster Al Capone out of $50,000, but wisely gave it back again.

Victor Lustig

Stanley Rifkin

In 1937, Edward Mueller began forging US dollar bills. Despite them being printed on the wrong sort of paper and with the wrong coloured ink, he was not caught for ten years.

In 1980, Stanley Rifkin stole more than $10 million by computer fraud. It only took him thirty seconds to steal, but he was sentenced to eight years in jail.

A machine called The Turk which could play chess made a fortune for its owners between 1769 and 1838 by winning games against expert chess players. It was later discovered that a series of chess-playing dwarfs were hidden inside the machine.

Never give a sucker an even break

The nineteenth century American, Phineas Taylor Barnum, was the world's greatest showman. He exhibited real curiosities and freaks, but many of his attractions were ridiculous frauds. He would exhibit anything as long as his gullible customers paid their entrance fees to see them.

'A cherry-coloured cat' - which was the colour of black cherries!

'A horse with its tail where its head should be'!

'A Fiji Mermaid' - which was made up from a stuffed fish and stuffed monkey.

In many countries, forgers of coins could be put to death. At the time of Elizabeth I in England, if a forger escaped the death penalty, he could be fined, put in the stocks, have his nostrils slit and have his ears lopped off.

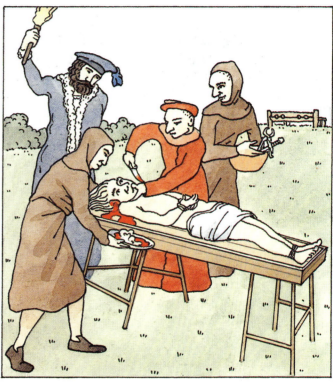

In 1928, Liberian president Charles King was reelected with a majority of 600,000 votes. There were only 15,000 voters in the whole country.

Hans van Meegeren is known as the greatest art forger of all time. His brilliant fakes earned him a fortune, and now, even if they are discovered to be fakes, they are still valuable because he is so famous.

President Ferdinand Marcos of the Philippines diverted $10 billion belonging to his people to his own foreign bank accounts between 1965 and 1988.

As a young man, Michelangelo sold new works of art as antiques. He buried new statues in soil to stain them and make them look old.

WARNING - THESE PAGES ARE ESPECIALLY HORRIBLE

MURDER MOST FOUL

It may seem odd, but according to the law in most countries, deliberately killing someone isn't necessarily illegal. For example, during a war, soldiers may kill enemy soldiers without breaking the law. But deliberately killing someone without a legal reason to do so is called MURDER.
Some murders are worse than others.

There was a real Count Dracula - Vlad Dracul who ruled the small country of Wallachia from 1456 to 1476. He didn't suck blood, but he liked to watch his victims being impaled on spikes while he dined. He was known as 'Vlad the Impaler'.

Cannibalism

In 1928, New Yorker Albert Fish killed 10 year old Grace Budd. He cooked and ate parts of her body with carrots and onions. At his trial he said that he was fond of children.

German Fritz Haarmann killed 50 young men between 1919 and 1924 by biting through their throats. He sold the bodies on the black market as beef or pork.

8

Between 1866 and 1900, twenty thousand American men died from illegal gunshot wounds. The famous Boot Hill Cemetery was so called because most of its occupants had died with their boots on. Many died in street gunfights.

In 1611, Countess Erzsébet of Hungary was tried for the torture and murder of 610 people. She bathed in her victims' blood in order to preserve her beauty.

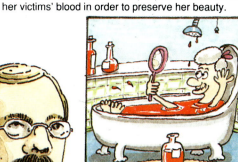

Dr Harvey Crippen

In 1910, Dr Harvey Crippen murdered his wife. His crime was discovered when police found pieces of her flesh buried in Crippen's cellar. Crippen was captured on board a ship bound for Canada, with his mistress who was disguised as a schoolboy. The ship's Captain recognised him and radioed his whereabouts to the London police - the first time radio had been used to capture a criminal. Crippen was arrested as he landed in America. He was later hanged.

Gilles de Rais was accused of the torture and murder of 300 children in France between 1432 and 1440. He was a keen alchemist and needed the blood for his attempts to turn iron into gold.

Tamerlane the Great was a Mongol warlord who built pyramids of the heads of his enemies. He is said to have killed anyone who told him a joke he'd heard before.

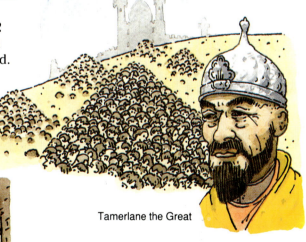

Tamerlane the Great

In London in 1888, at least seven women were brutally murdered by the same person. A letter in red ink boasting about the murders and signed 'Jack the Ripper' was sent to a London newspaper. Jack was never caught, and there have been many different theories about his identity - he was a famous doctor, or he was related to Queen Victoria, or he was even a woman - Jill the Ripper!

ASSASSINATIONS

The murder of important political or religious leaders is called assassination. Political assassinations can lead to riots and even wars where thousands of people may be killed or injured.

In 1914, Archduke Ferdinand of Austria was assassinated by a group of Serbian nationalists called the Black Hand Gang. His assassination was the spark that started the First World War and led to a further 20 million deaths.

Four United States presidents have been assassinated.

Abraham Lincoln was shot whilst watching a play at a Washington theatre by John Wilkes Booth on 14 April 1865. Booth broke his shin when he jumped on to the stage to escape. He went on the run for twelve days and was then captured in Virginia and shot dead.

James Garfield was shot whilst walking to a train by Charles J. Guiteau on 2 July 1881. He died of his wounds on 19 September. Guiteau was hanged a year later.

William McKinley was shot by Leon Czolgosz on 6 September 1901. He died eight days later. Czolgosz was beaten by soldiers and then arrested. A few weeks later, he went to the electric chair.

John Fitzgerald Kennedy was shot in the head by Lee Harvey Oswald on 20 November 1963 from a school book depository. Oswald was later shot and killed whilst on live television.

Roman Emperor Julius Caesar was stabbed more than twenty times by a group of his former colleagues on 15 March 44 BC.

In 1968, the black civil rights and religious leader Martin Luther King was assassinated because of his beliefs.

Roman orator and statesman Cicero wanted a return to a Republican Rome but was opposed by a Roman senator called Mark Anthony. Cicero was assassinated in 43 BC. Mark Anthony's wife stuck pins in his tongue because she had been jealous of his powers of oratory.

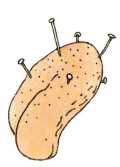

The French revolutionary and leading member of the Jacobin party Jean-Paul Marat was assassinated in his bath by a girl called Charlotte Corday in 1793. She was a supporter of the Girondin party, which opposed the violent Jacobin policies.

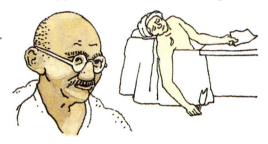

Mahatma Gandhi helped end British Rule in India but was assassinated at a garden party by one of his countrymen in 1948.

Most of the Russian royal family was slaughtered by the Communist revolutionaries in 1918 and buried in a secret grave. This grave was later discovered, and in 1993 the bodies were identified as the Russian royal family from traces of DNA in the bones.

Infamous names

The Hashishin were eleventh century Persian religious fanatics who murdered after taking the drug hashish. The word 'assassin' comes from their name.

'Mafia' comes from the Italian word for scrubland. Sicilian outlaws used to live in the 'mafia' hill country.

'Hatchet men' were nineteenth century Chinese gangsters called the Tongs who killed their victims with hatchets.

The word 'thug' comes from 'Thuggee' a Hindu sect (c.1500-1830) which worshipped Kali the goddess of destruction. Members of the sect strangled and robbed up to two million travellers.

GOTCHA!

In the past, ordinary citizens often had responsibility for law enforcement. For instance, in ninth century England, the law said that people must join in any 'hue and cry' and chase suspected criminals. If necessary, soldiers were used to back them up. But soldiers are trained to fight wars and they can be too rough for law enforcement work. So modern societies have developed special law enforcement agencies called police forces.

Wyatt Earp is perhaps the most famous of the Wild West Sheriffs. He was sheriff in the town of Wichita, Texas. In fact, he was not much better than his fellow townsmen. After two years as sheriff he was arrested, fined and fired for disturbing the peace!

The first constables were men who had responsibility for looking after the horses of the Roman Emperors.

The Russian KGB was formed in 1954. For many years it was the largest secret police and spying organisation in the world. At one time it controlled 300,000 border guards as well as a much larger number of other agents.

Gotcha! firsts

Catching criminals by studying their handwriting was first practised by the Romans in AD 500.

The Pinkertons detective agency was set up in the USA in 1850. They were the first to use 'mug-shot' wanted posters.

The first police car was used in Ohio in 1899.

The first lie detector was introduced in the USA in 1921.

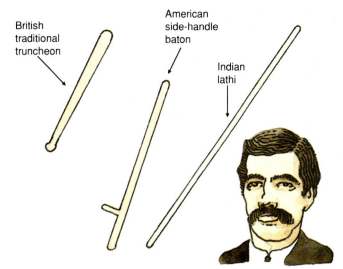

Marshall Tom Smith tried to keep the peace in the lawless Kansas cow-town of Abilene with just his fists. He lasted only five months before being shot dead in November 1870.

The first uniformed English police were the Bow Street Runners founded by the magistrate and writer Henry Fielding between 1748 and 1753. They were paid rewards for catching criminals. In 1829 they were replaced by the modern police force. The new policemen were called 'peelers' or 'bobbies' after their founder Sir Robert Peel.

The 'Mounties', or Royal Canadian Mounted Police, often tracked criminals for weeks through the huge forests of North West Canada. Their motto is 'The Mounties always get their man'.

Kangaroo courts (illegal trials) were common in the Wild West. The name comes from the way the judges 'jumped' to conclusions. Such trials often ended in a lynching (an illegal hanging).

ON TRIAL

When someone is accused of a crime a trial is held to find out if they are guilty or innocent and to decide on a punishment. In many early societies cases were 'tried' by kings, lords or priests. Ordinary people appeared before them to ask them to settle disputes or punish wrongdoers. Nowadays magistrates try petty crimes. More serious crimes are tried by judges or other such experts. In the USA and Britain, serious crimes are tried in front of a judge and a jury. Trial by jury was first developed in ancient Greece. A jury is a group of ordinary citizens selected at random. Most countries also have some sort of supreme court which can alter the decisions of lesser courts. In the USA this is called the Supreme Court. In Britain it is the House of Lords.

During the seventeenth century in England, some men wore straws stuck in their shoe-buckles and were known as 'straw men'. This was to advertise their services, for a fee, as friendly witnesses.

In the Middle Ages, people who could read were treated as priests and received lesser sentences than ordinary citizens. In 1598, playwright Ben Jonson killed a man in a duel. Instead of being hanged he was merely given a small brand on his left thumb!

Judge Roy Bean (1825-1904) was a saloon-keeper and a Justice of the Peace in rough, tough West Texas. He was judge, jury and executioner combined, and had eccentric ideas about the law. He once fined a corpse $40 for carrying a concealed weapon!

The Romans divided citizens into two classes: *honestiores* and *humiliores*. *Honestiores* were rich and were treated gently by the law. *Humiliores* were poor and received harsher punishments. In most countries nowadays, all people are considered equal in the eyes of the law.

A jury may make a wrong decision on purpose because its members have been bribed or threatened. Greek courts had juries of 200 men to make it hard to corrupt them.

Trial by ordeal was common in the Middle Ages. In this type of trial it was assumed that God would show who was innocent and who was guilty.

Trial by combat
Accused and accuser would fight a trial by combat, using swords, knives or lances. The winner was declared innocent.

Trial by fire
The accused had to walk over red-hot ploughshares and pick up a hot iron bar. The hands and feet were wrapped up and examined three days later. If a blister larger than a walnut was found then the prisoner was guilty.

Trial by cheese
Priests were tried by fellow priests. Suspects were given a piece of cheese to eat. If they couldn't swallow it, they were considered guilty.

Trial by water
During the early Middle Ages the accused (often a witch) would be given holy water to drink and then tied up and thrown into a river. If they floated they were guilty and were executed. If they sank they were considered innocent, but they drowned anyway.

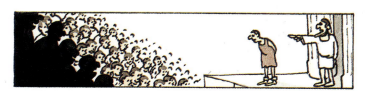

15

PRISON

Prisons have existed for at least 5,000 years. At first they were mainly used to hold hostages or prisoners awaiting trial. After trial, convicted prisoners suffered a variety of other often painful punishments.

During the eighteenth century, some European countries began to send convicts to prison colonies abroad as an alternative, and to save space in their own prisons. This was called transportation. At the same time prison reformers began to protest against executions and other harsh punishments. By 1800, new types of prison were being built. Inmates were treated better than before and loss of freedom became the main punishment. Inmates were encouraged to feel sorry, or penitent, about doing wrong. American prisons even became known as 'penitentiaries'.

Nick names

Criminals have invented many words for prison over the years.

Big house
Can
Chokey
Clanger
Clink
Cooler
Coop
Inside
Jug
Nick
Pen
Pokey
Quod
Slammer
Stir
Tronk

Old ships which were no longer seaworthy, called hulks, were often used as prisons. Many of the prisoners were waiting to be transported.

Between 1791 and 1853, about 45,000 Irish convicts were transported to Australia, as well as many thousands from England, Scotland and Wales.

Until recently, convicts wore special clothes which were easy to spot if they escaped.

American convicts wore striped suits. British prison uniforms were covered in arrow symbols.

Prisoners in America used to be chained together in 'chain-gangs' then taken out to do hard labour such as repairing roads or breaking rocks.

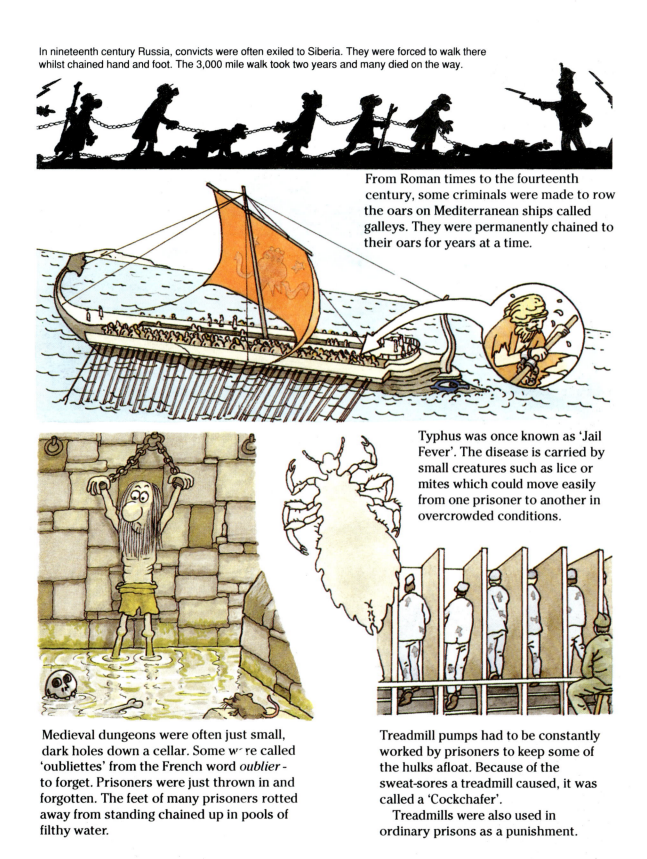

In nineteenth century Russia, convicts were often exiled to Siberia. They were forced to walk there whilst chained hand and foot. The 3,000 mile walk took two years and many died on the way.

From Roman times to the fourteenth century, some criminals were made to row the oars on Mediterranean ships called galleys. They were permanently chained to their oars for years at a time.

Typhus was once known as 'Jail Fever'. The disease is carried by small creatures such as lice or mites which could move easily from one prisoner to another in overcrowded conditions.

Medieval dungeons were often just small, dark holes down a cellar. Some were called 'oubliettes' from the French word *oublier* - to forget. Prisoners were just thrown in and forgotten. The feet of many prisoners rotted away from standing chained up in pools of filthy water.

Treadmill pumps had to be constantly worked by prisoners to keep some of the hulks afloat. Because of the sweat-sores a treadmill caused, it was called a 'Cockchafer'.

Treadmills were also used in ordinary prisons as a punishment.

ESCAPE

It is illegal for convicts or prisoners awaiting trial to escape or try to escape. Even so, many attempt it because of their strong desire for freedom. Escaping is often considered worse than many of the crimes for which a prisoner may have been convicted. This means that a recaptured convict may have several years added to a sentence, or even face death.

Escaper's tool kit - file to file through bars, spade for tunnelling, knotted sheets to act as a rope, bolster to look like sleeping prisoner, hand made clothes, false passport, lock pick, wig for disguise.

Prisons are often built on islands because this makes escape doubly difficult. Alcatraz island in San Francisco Bay was a grim maximum security prison from 1934 to 1962. Twenty-three attempted to escape, but all were killed or recaptured except for five, who were presumed drowned. Alcatraz is now a museum.

Napoleon on the ship *Bellerophon*, bound for Saint Helena as a prisoner of war.

The defeated French Emperor Napoleon Bonaparte escaped from the Mediterranean island of Elba in 1815. He raised an army and marched to Paris. After his defeat at the battle of Waterloo he was exiled to the remote Atlantic island of Saint Helena. There was no escape from this tiny island. He died there in 1821.

In 1880, Billy the Kid escaped from Fort Sumner County Jail even though he was handcuffed and had his legs shackled.

Devil's Island was a famous French penal colony off the coast of South America. One prisoner, named Gerardin, faked the symptoms of leprosy by cutting off his fingers. He was removed to a nearby leper colony island and then he escaped to Brazil.

Unfortunately, it was then found that he really did have leprosy. The Brazilian authorities built him a small prison of his own.

The Tower of London was reserved for the king's enemies. The twelfth century Bishop of Durham, Ranulf Flambard, was the first political prisoner to be imprisoned in the tower. He was also the first to escape after arranging for a rope to be smuggled into the tower inside a wine cask.

Prisoners have often been freed during popular uprisings. The Bastille State Prison in Paris was stormed by an enraged mob of peasants in 1789. Though only seven prisoners were released, this symbolic act helped start the French Revolution.

In 1919, the Irish freedom fighter Eamon de Valera escaped from Lincoln Jail using keys smuggled into the jail hidden inside Christmas cakes. He fled to the USA, later returning to Ireland to become Prime Minister, and then President.

WARNING - THESE PAGES ARE ESPECIALLY HORRIBLE

CHAMBER OF HORRORS

'Torture' comes from a Latin word meaning 'to twist'. It was once standard practice and was used to extract confessions. A skilful torturer knew how to keep his victim alive for as long as possible while inflicting the maximum amount of pain. Torture was made illegal in England in 1640 and is now forbidden under international law, although several regimes still make use of it.

A chained prisoner on trial in nineteenth century China

Ancient Chinese water tortures
There were many different tortures involving water.

The victim was tied down underneath a steady drip of water on his forehead which drove him insane.

Bamboo shoots were fed to a victim who was then forced to drink. Over the next few days, the shoots would grow through the stomach and emerge from the skin.

The victim would be tied down over a bed of bamboo shoots. The shoots were watered and would grow up through the victim.

Water would be pumped down the victim's throat until his stomach burst.

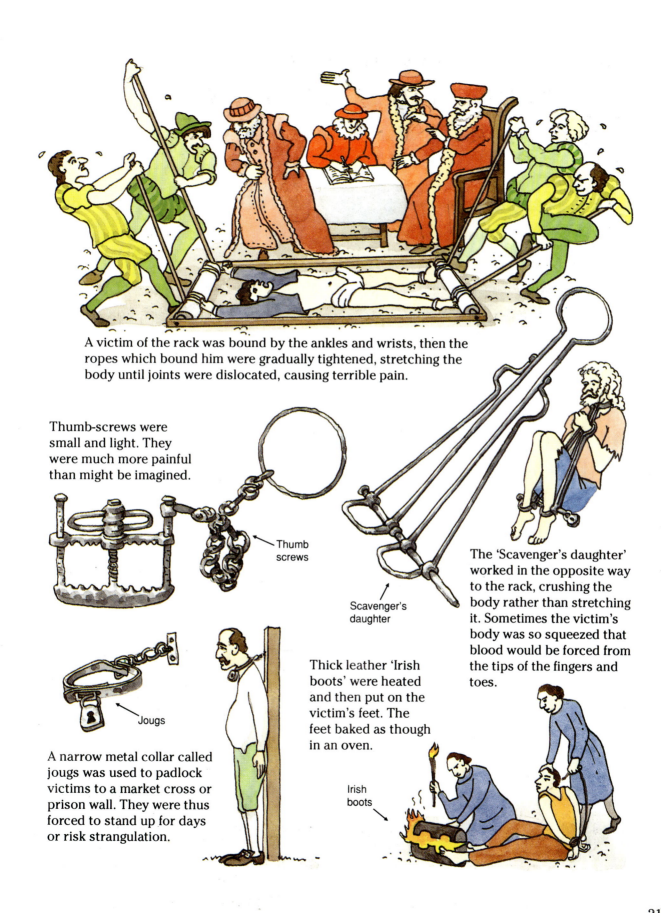

A victim of the rack was bound by the ankles and wrists, then the ropes which bound him were gradually tightened, stretching the body until joints were dislocated, causing terrible pain.

Thumb-screws were small and light. They were much more painful than might be imagined.

Thumb screws

Scavenger's daughter

The 'Scavenger's daughter' worked in the opposite way to the rack, crushing the body rather than stretching it. Sometimes the victim's body was so squeezed that blood would be forced from the tips of the fingers and toes.

Jougs

A narrow metal collar called jougs was used to padlock victims to a market cross or prison wall. They were thus forced to stand up for days or risk strangulation.

Thick leather 'Irish boots' were heated and then put on the victim's feet. The feet baked as though in an oven.

Irish boots

Branding with a hot iron was a common punishment, or ownership mark. Foreheads, cheeks and fingers were the most usual places to be branded.

H = Harlot or Heretic
D = Drunkard
S = Slave
M = Murderer
T = Thief

PUBLIC PUNISHMENTS

In the past many punishments involved public humiliation. This demonstrated the power of the law to the people who passed by, as well as being very unpleasant for the wrongdoer. These sorts of punishment were considered very important in medieval Europe. An English town of the period would not be allowed to hold a market if it did not maintain a pillory. Even small villages might have a ducking stool and a whipping post.

Ducking stools were chairs on the end of a long pole. Victims such as cheating tradesmen, harlots and witches were tied to the chair and lowered into a pond or river until they nearly drowned.

Scold's bridle

Nagging wives were sometimes made to wear a 'scold's bridle' to hold their tongues.

Drunkard's cloak

Drunkards in New England, USA, were forced to wear a 'drunkard's cloak'. This was a barrel with holes cut out for arms, legs and head. It was meant to make them look silly.

WITCHES AND HERETICS

Most primitive cultures have a fear of bad magic. This fear lingered in Europe and America into the recent past and resulted in the persecution of people, especially old women, who were thought to be witches. Witches were often burned at the stake, as were heretics. Heretics were people who questioned orthodox versions of Christianity. Some medieval heretics were hacked to pieces with an axe.

The Spanish Inquisition persecuted Moslems, Jews and Protestants. Thousands of people were burned to death after being convicted of religious crimes and then sentenced at a public ceremony called an *Auto da fé*, or 'Act of Faith'. Victims of burning were often strangled as an act of mercy before the flames consumed them.

The Iron Maiden was used for executions by church officials in medieval Germany. The spikes on the inside of the lid pierced the victim when the lid was closed. The spikes were sometimes arranged so that two of them pierced the victim's eyes.

Iroquois Native Americans executed witches by ripping off their skin and tying them to anthills.

In 1589, Frenchman Peter Stube was convicted of being a werewolf. His skin was torn off with red-hot pincers as a punishment.

In medieval Germany, blasphemers might have their tongues ripped out with red-hot pincers.

In Salem, Massachusetts, in 1692, two girls aged nine and eleven made accusations of witchcraft. The idea caught on and soon a number of girls had accused more than three hundred people of witchcraft. Twenty of their victims were executed. One of them, Giles Cory, was pressed to death with heavy weights. He was eighty years old.

Women convicted of crimes for which a man might be beheaded were often burnt to death instead. This was because burning was thought to be a more decent way for women to die as it did not involve any cutting of their bodies.

In 1471, a Swiss cockerel was found guilty of laying an egg 'in defiance of natural law'. It was burnt at the stake as a devil.

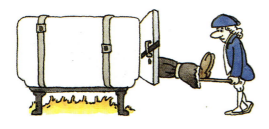

From 1651 to 1660, at least 2,000 women were burnt as witches in Silesia in what is now Poland. They were roasted in huge ovens.

OFF WITH THEIR HEADS!

The execution of wrongdoers is called capital punishment, from the Latin word *caput* meaning 'head'. In the past, decapitation, or death by removal of the head, was considered the most dignified way to die, and was often reserved for the nobility. Common people were more likely to be hanged.

When the guillotine was introduced by M. Guillotin in 1792, decapitation became very efficient. The guillotine was a heavy blade, raised between two poles and set at an angle, which fell on the victim's neck when released. Thousands of French aristocrats were executed with this device during the French Revolution.

The Sansons were a family of French executioners. Charles-Henri Sanson worked for the French revolutionaries. He decapitated over 4,000 people during his career. He sometimes sold their fat as a remedy for rheumatism.

Old ladies called *tricoteuses*, which is French for knitters, sat by the guillotine during the French Revolution. They knitted to pass the time between executions.

The principal of the guillotine has been known for two thousand years. The Chinese fitted a blade to a swinging tree trunk.

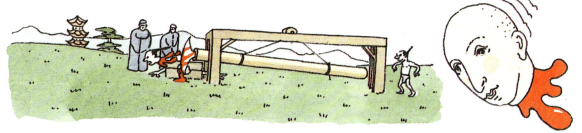

Blood from a decapitated body may jet several feet into the air.

When Mary Queen of Scots was executed, her wig fell from her head. The head rolled on the floor like a ball.

In Germany, decapitation with a sword was a privilege reserved for aristocrats. There, and in some other countries, people who were to be executed by the sword knelt upright. Skilled executioners would slice off the head with one blow.

Executioner Jack Ketch was notorious for his cruelty and inefficiency. He took five blows of the axe to execute the Duke of Monmouth. The head was then sewed back on so that Monmouth's portrait could be painted.

Block   v   Guillotine

An axe-man had to have a perfect aim to be able to decapitate with a single blow. The victim had to be held in exactly the right position.

The guillotine held the victim's neck securely as the blade flashed through it. This helped to give a neat cut every time.

SENTENCED TO DEATH

Throughout history there have been many forms of execution apart from decapitation. In the past many types of execution were meant to be horribly unpleasant.

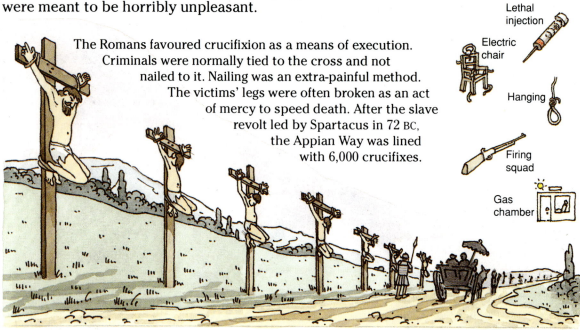

The Romans favoured crucifixion as a means of execution. Criminals were normally tied to the cross and not nailed to it. Nailing was an extra-painful method. The victims' legs were often broken as an act of mercy to speed death. After the slave revolt led by Spartacus in 72 BC, the Appian Way was lined with 6,000 crucifixes.

Some modern forms of execution

- Lethal injection
- Electric chair
- Hanging
- Firing squad
- Gas chamber

The Moors executed Christians by throwing them into snake pits.

The Anglo-Saxons executed traitors by shooting arrows into them.

The Aztecs roasted prisoners alive over fires of chilli peppers.

The Inuit left prisoners tied up on the ice to be killed by polar bears or the cold.

In ancient Egypt criminals were thrown to the sacred Nile crocodiles.

Hanging was a popular entertainment. In 1807, 40,000 people crammed into a London square to watch the double hanging of two criminals called Holloway and Haggerty. Many of the spectators were trampled to death.

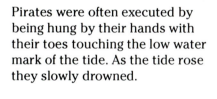

Pirates were often executed by being hung by their hands with their toes touching the low water mark of the tide. As the tide rose they slowly drowned.

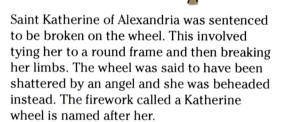

Saint Katherine of Alexandria was sentenced to be broken on the wheel. This involved tying her to a round frame and then breaking her limbs. The wheel was said to have been shattered by an angel and she was beheaded instead. The firework called a Katherine wheel is named after her.

The Chinese practised a form of execution called 'Death by a Thousand Cuts'. The victim was killed as slowly as possible by a myriad small cuts all over his body.

Hanging, drawing and quartering was a punishment reserved for English traitors. They were first pulled through the town on a wooden frame behind a horse. Then they were hung until half dead. After that they were taken down and their intestines were pulled out before their eyes. This treatment finally killed them. Their arms, legs and head were then chopped up and sent to be displayed in the four corners of the kingdom.

THE FUTURE

Most of the punishments described in this book have been abolished. But crimes are still committed and criminals are still punished. In the future new technologies may make our lives more comfortable, but they will not stop crime. Advances in technology will lead to new types of crime and new forms of control and punishment for those who break the law.

Semi-automatic police such as Robocop or Judge Dredd are popular fantasies, but advances in bio-cybernetics may make such creations possible.

Theft prevention

'Intelligent' houses will detect and capture burglars.

Cars will wait in secure garages and only come when they're called.

Voice-activated credit cards will make fraud more difficult.

Electronic tagging of criminals so their movements can be checked has already been introduced experimentally in California.

Computers will soon be able to store information on the genetic codes of entire populations. Every individual except identical twins has a unique code. It will be easy to identify who has left any small flakes of skin or drops of body fluids such as blood at the scene of a crime.

She did it!

She did it!

There are more laws now than ever before. If the number of laws were reduced there would be fewer crimes to commit!

Ordinary citizens may form vigilante groups such as the New York Guardian Angels if crime levels continue to rise.

Perhaps the best solution to crime in the future will have nothing to do with technology. If people live in small communities where they know their neighbours, crime becomes much more unlikely.

31

DISASTER!

Are you male or female?
Dead women tend to float on their backs. Dead men tend to float on their fronts.

FLOOD!

All life on Earth needs water. Most centres of population are near the sea or a lake or river so as to have a ready supply of water. But although water is essential for life it can also be very dangerous. Stories of catastrophic floods caused by angry gods are as old as civilisation and common to cultures all over the world.

Major flood disasters
c. 3500 BC The Great Flood
1219 Norway, lake overflow, 36,000 drowned
1362 Holland, Great Drowning, 30,000 drowned
1421 Failed dykes, Holland, 100,000 drowned
1530 Failed dykes, Holland, 400,000 drowned
1642 River embankments destroyed by rebels, Kaifong, China, 300,000 drowned
1876 Storm surge, Ganges and Brahmaputra estuaries, India, 200,000 drowned
1887 Hwang Ho, China, 1.5 million drowned
1896 Japan, tidal wave, 27,000 drowned
1931 Hwang Ho river, China, possibly worst flood ever. Several millions drowned
1938 Chinese dam destroyed to halt invading Japanese, 500,000 Chinese drowned

The Hwang Ho (Yellow River) is called China's Sorrow. Its banks have been built up 8 metres above the surrounding plain, where millions of Chinese live. When the banks burst, as they often do, huge numbers of farms and people are washed away. During a typical flood, an area of China the size of Britain is under water.

In 1927, aircraft flew over the Mississippi broadcasting a flood warning. Many people had never seen an aeroplane before. They thought it was the voice of God announcing the end of the world.

In 1929, archaeologists uncovered a thick layer of river mud under the ancient city of Ur (in modern Iraq). This was dated to about 3500 BC - about the right date for the Bible story of Noah's Ark and the Flood.

In 1362, the North Sea flooded Holland. Thirty thousand people were killed. It was called the *Grote Mandrenke* (Great Drowning). Over a million Dutch people have drowned since AD 1000.

The cemetery of Dunwich, Suffolk, was washed away by the sea in 1740. Odd bones, skulls and complete skeletons were washed through the drowned streets of the town.

A tsunami, or tidal wave, caused by the Krakatoa volcano in 1883, carried a ship 3 km inland and into the jungle on a nearby island.

The River Arno flooded Florence, Italy, in November 1966. Half a million tonnes of mud and slime were deposited in the ancient streets in a single night.

One of the oddest floods occurred in Boston, USA, on 15 January 1919. A storage tank containing 4.5 million litres of black treacle burst and sent a huge wave of treacle pouring through the streets. Twenty-one people were killed.

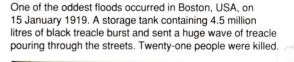

FIRE!

Peking Man was the first human to use fire, about 350,000 years ago. Fire was used for warmth and cooking. Cooking helped to make food safe and edible, and is said to be the greatest hygiene invention of all time. Because fire was once so difficult to produce, villages in the ancient world kept public fires which were never allowed to go out.

Following the earthquake of 1906 in San Francisco a fire was started by someone cooking breakfast. It burned for three days and destroyed 28,000 buildings. Because the earthquake had destroyed the water supply some waiters tried to put out the flames with wine!

The Chicago fire of 1871 is said to have been started by a cow which kicked over an oil lamp. Eighteen thousand buildings were destroyed and two hundred and fifty people were killed.

Emperor Augustus started the first Fire Brigade in 27 BC. However, Rome was still destroyed by fire in AD 64. The crazed Emperor Nero is said to have carried on playing his lyre as Rome fell around him.

Major fire disasters

97 BC-AD 696	Library of Alexandria destroyed
AD 4	Great Fire of Rome, hundreds burned
1570	Moscow, 200,000 burned
1666	Great Fire of London, 8 died
1769	Brescia, Italy, 300 died
1824	Cairo, 4,000 died
1857	Tokyo, fire after earthquake, 107,000 died
1863	La Campania Church, Chile, 2,500 died
1871	Peshtigo, Wisconsin, forest fire, 1,500 died
1871	Great Fire of Chicago, 250 died
1906	San Francisco, 700 died
1918	Minnesota, forest fire, 800 died
1923	Tokyo, after earthquake, 40,000 died
1934	Hokodate, Japan, 1,500 died
1942	Coconut Grove Club, Boston, 491 died
1983	Great Australian Bushfire, 200,000 sheep and 77 people died

Some fires start naturally. The great Australian bushfire of 1983 devastated an area of about 8,000 sq km. One couple survived the passing firestorm by turning the garden hose on their car and sheltering inside.

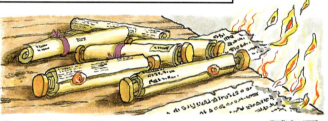

The great Library of Alexandria in Egypt was destroyed by a series of fires between 97 BC and AD 696. Thousands of priceless ancient manuscripts were lost.

An earthquake in Tokyo in 1923 caused winds to whip up the small fires which had started in damaged buildings. Traditional Japanese buildings of that period were built mainly of wood and paper because of the danger of earthquakes. Forty thousand died in the swift flames.

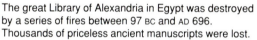

The Great Fire of London started in 1666 in a bakery in Pudding Lane. It raged for three days, destroying most of the city. King Charles II helped with the fire-fighting. Twenty thousand people were made homeless, but only eight died.

People have tried to explain earthquakes in many different ways:

Inuits believed that earthquakes were caused by a giant whale twitching its tail.

Some native Americans believed that a giant tortoise held up the Earth. It sometimes moved.

The Greeks thought that the god Atlas stood on the edge of the world holding up the sky. He occasionally stumbled.

EARTHQUAKE!

The surface of the Earth is covered by a layer of hard rock called the crust. Underneath the crust is a layer of molten rock. The solid crust is not in one piece. It is made up of chunks like pieces of a giant jigsaw puzzle. These chunks are called tectonic plates. They may be thousands of miles across and they float about very slowly on the molten rock below. Earthquakes mainly occur along fault lines where the tectonic plates rub against each other. There may be as many as a million earthquakes every year. Most are too small to be noticed without instruments, but some are immensely powerful. During four thousand years of recorded history, earthquakes are estimated to have caused the deaths of more than seven million people.

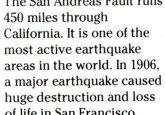

The San Andreas Fault runs 450 miles through California. It is one of the most active earthquake areas in the world. In 1906, a major earthquake caused huge destruction and loss of life in San Francisco.

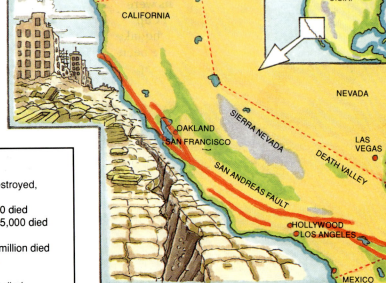

Major earthquake disasters
1450 BC Italy, thousands dead
AD 365 Egypt, Pharos lighthouse destroyed, 50,000 died
526 Syria, Antioch buried, 250,000 died
856 Greece, Corinth destroyed, 45,000 died
893 India, 180,000 died
1202 Eastern Mediterranean, one million died
1556 Shensi, China, 830,000 died
1692 Jamaica, 93,000 died
1703 Edo (Tokyo), Japan, 200,000 died
1755 Lisbon, Portugal, up to 100,000 died
1906 San Francisco, USA, 700 died
1908 Messina, Italy, 160,000 died
1920 Kansu province, China, 180,000 died
1923 Tokyo and Yokahama, Japan, 143,000 died
1964 Alaska, most powerful earthquake recorded
1976 Tangshan province, China, 242,000 died

During the Tokyo earthquake of 1923, a Mrs Chichester-Smith was having a bath in her hotel. The hotel collapsed and she fell to the street in her bath - without a drop of water being spilled.

The power of earthquakes is measured on an instrument called a seismograph according to a scale devised by an American called Charles Richter. The most powerful earthquake ever recorded was the 'Good Friday' earthquake in Alaska in 1964. It measured 8.9 on the Richter scale, and it was equal in power to the explosion of 140 million tonnes of TNT.

In 1755, Lisbon was hit by an earthquake. Sixty thousand people died in the first few minutes of destruction. Waves caused by the earthquake made ships rock free from their moorings one thousand miles away in England.

On the night of 21 June 1990, many Iranians were watching Brazil versus Scotland in a World Cup football match on television. A sudden earthquake killed 40,000 in their beds. There would have been many more deaths if everyone had been asleep.

Huge cracks in the ground appeared during the 1692 earthquake in Jamaica. Many people who fell into the cracks were crushed when they closed up.

Some animals, such as dogs and pheasants, are more sensitive to vibrations than humans. They may be warned of an earthquake by tiny vibrations in the ground. The Chinese have become expert at observing animals and can now often predict when an earthquake is going to start.

An earthquake which struck the Eastern Mediterranean in 1202 may have taken a million lives. In the city of Baalbek, rockfalls killed 200 rhubarb gatherers.

VOLCANOES

The molten rock beneath the Earth's crust sometimes escapes through the crust to the surface. The places where this happens are called volcanoes. Often the molten rock escapes gradually, but sometimes it erupts with immense destructive force.

As many as 300,000 people have been killed by volcanoes since AD 1400.

Major volcano disasters
1500 BC Santorini caused tidal wave which may have destroyed the Minoan civilisation
477 BC Italy, Mount Etna, thousands died
AD 79 Italy, Vesuvius destroys Pompeii, 15,000 killed.
150 Tampo Island, New Zealand, probably the greatest eruption in the last 2,000 years
1631 Vesuvius, 18,000 died
1755 Mount Etna again, 36,000 died
1793 Miyi-Yama, Java, 53,000 died
1794 Tungurahua, Ecuador, 40,000 died
1815 Tambora, near Java, 11,994 died
1883 Krakatoa, up to 50,000 died
1902 Mont Pelée, 30,000 died
1985 Nevada del Ruiz, Columbia, mud flow, 23,000 killed

Mount Vesuvius in Southern Italy erupted in AD 79. The nearby town of Pompeii was buried under millions of tonnes of volcanic ash. Fifteen thousand people died. The ash set hard around their bodies forming a 'mould'. Hundreds of years later after the bodies had rotted away, plaster was poured into some of these almost empty spaces. When the ash was chipped away the plaster casts showed the exact shapes of people in their death agony.

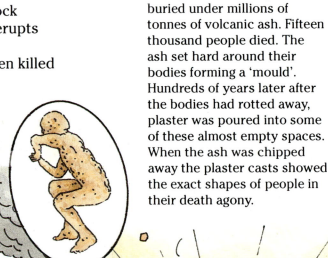

A Roman belief was that Mount Etna in Italy was the prison of the giant Enceladus. His struggles to escape caused eruptions.

The word volcano comes from Vulcan, the blacksmith of the Roman gods. His home was said to be in a volcano in Sicily - called Vulcano.

The largest known volcano is Olympus Mons on the planet Mars. It is three times as tall as Mount Everest.

The present Mediterranean island of Santorini is the remains of a previous island called Thera. It exploded in about 1500 BC, causing a tidal wave which destroyed the civilization of the nearby island of Crete. The drowning of Crete is thought by some archaeologists to explain the story of the sunken island of Atlantis.

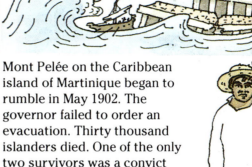

Pneumonoultramicroscopicsilicovolcanoconiosis is the name given to the effects of breathing the poison gas given off by volcanoes.

Mont Pelée on the Caribbean island of Martinique began to rumble in May 1902. The governor failed to order an evacuation. Thirty thousand islanders died. One of the only two survivors was a convict called Auguste Ciparis who was protected by his prison cell. He later toured with a circus as 'The Man who Escaped Hell'.

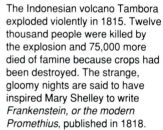

The Indonesian volcano Tambora exploded violently in 1815. Twelve thousand people were killed by the explosion and 75,000 more died of famine because crops had been destroyed. The strange, gloomy nights are said to have inspired Mary Shelley to write *Frankenstein, or the modern Prometheus*, published in 1818.

In 1883, the Indonesian island of Krakatoa suddenly exploded. The rumble was heard up to 3,000 km away. This was possibly the loudest noise ever heard. Fine ash shot 50 km into the upper atmosphere, making the Moon appear blue for many months afterwards.

Hurricane comes from the name of the Arawak Indian god Huracan.

Typhoon comes from the Chinese *tai fung* meaning 'big wind'.

Cyclone comes from the Greek word *kuklos* meaning 'a circle'.

STORM!

Some of the Ancients thought that the wind was the breath of gods. Others believed winds were caused by the flapping wings of god-like eagles on the edge of the world. Now we know that winds are moving air masses powered by the heat of the Sun. The most powerful winds can reach speeds of over 200 mph, or even 400 mph near the centre of tornadoes.

To survive a hurricane, get into a hole or ditch below ground. Avoid open-plan buildings such as swimming pools or sports halls. These sorts of buildings usually suffer the worst wind damage.

In 1780, during the American War of Independence, hurricanes broke up the British, French, Spanish and Dutch fleets. These fleets had sailed to America to attack and re-take the newly independent former colonies.

In 1274, the Chinese Emperor Kublai Khan set out with 1,000 ships to invade Japan, but a typhoon, which the Japanese call the 'Kamikaze' or 'Divine Wind', destroyed his ships and 13,000 men. In 1281, he tried again but another typhoon struck. He lost nearly 4,000 ships and 100,000 soldiers. He gave up.

The biggest storm in British history took place in 1703. Thousands of trees blew down, whole lead roofs of churches flew off, and at least 8,000 lives were lost at sea. Four hundred windmills spun so fast that their sails caught fire.

Major storm disasters
- 1274 Sea of Japan, typhoon destroys Chinese fleet, 13,000 died
- 1281 Sea of Japan, typhoon destroys Chinese fleet, 99,997 died
- 1703 Britain, the Great Storm, over 8,000 died
- 1737 Bengal, storm and sea surge, 300,000 died
- 1780 Caribbean hurricanes 25,000 died
- 1789 India, cyclone caused three huge waves, 300,000 died
- 1839 Coringa, India, cyclone caused floods, 300,000 died
- 1876 Backarunge, India, cyclone, 100,000 died
- 1900 Galveston, USA, 6,000 died
- 1933-34 Dustbowl storms USA
- 1959 Japan, 210 kph winds, one million homeless, 5,100 died
- 1969 Greatest US storm, 320 kph winds, 300 died
- 1970 Bangladesh cyclone and sea surge, up to 500,000 died
- 1991 Bangladesh, cyclone and sea surge, ten million homeless, many died

The Dust Bowl storms of 1933-34 in the midwest of the USA caused huge destruction of farmland. Millions of tonnes of soil blew away, some of the soil being carried as far as New York. The dust storms were called 'Black Blizzards'.

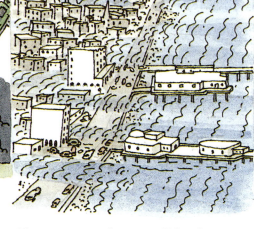

Winds which swirl in tight circles are called tornadoes or twisters. In 1931 a tornado in Minnesota lifted an 83 tonne train 25 metres into the air. When if fell, many of the passengers were killed.

Hurricanes can be up to 300 miles across. One of America's worst hurricanes occurred in 1900. Three thousand houses were destroyed in Galveston, Texas. Six thousand people were killed. An estimated two billion tonnes of water flooded the city.

Madness

The insistent cold Mistral wind of Southern France is reputed to drive people mad.

In Italy, the Scirocco is a stifling hot wind from the Sahara. It causes lethargy, insanity and suicide.

A 'simoom' is the Arabic name for a violent wind which raises maddening sandstorms in North Africa.

What to do if you're caught in a blizzard

Find shelter.

Don't move about or stamp your feet. This uses up energy. Frostbite is better than death!

Huddle together for warmth and don't risk going for help.

Stay awake. Don't go to sleep if you get drowsy. You may never wake up!

ICE AND SNOW

Snow rarely falls in warm climates. Since all the early civilisations grew up in warm southern climates, there is little mention of snow in documents which have survived from the ancient world. However experience from the recent past suggests that throughout history glaciers, avalanches, blizzards and hail storms have all caused many disasters. Avalanches have been particularly dangerous because they strike suddenly. Mountain communities throughout the world continue to suffer from avalanches to this day. Blizzards cover wider areas but are more dangerous to livestock left in the fields and to travellers caught between settlements.

There was a Little Ice Age from about 1550 to 1850 when rivers such as the Thames froze over every winter. Frost Fairs (annual markets) were held on the Thames ice until 1814, when the ice suddenly gave way and sent hundreds of fair-goers plunging to a watery doom.

Two types of avalanche

Dust avalanches of fresh, heavy snow slide down mountains at speeds of up to 200 mph. A surge of air pressure is created in front of the fast moving wall of snow which is almost as dangerous as the snow itself.

Ground avalanches of wet snow rarely travel more than 60 mph, but forces of up to 100 tons per square yard have been reported.

Ice wars

The Russians have often relied on ice and snow to repel invaders. In 1812 Napoleon's army of half a million men was reduced to just 50,000 by the harsh sub-zero temperatures of the Russian winter.

When Hannibal attacked Rome in 218 BC he took his army through the Alps. He lost 18,000 men and several war elephants through avalanches.

Ice was later used as a weapon in the Alps during the First World War. Avalanches were deliberately started to sweep away advancing troops. Eighty thousand soldiers died this way.

Major ice and snow disasters
218 BC Alps, avalanches devastated Hannibal's army, 18,000 died
1499 Alps, mercenary destroyed, 400 died
1888 Beheri, India, hailstones, 246 died
1812 Eastern Europe, Napoleon's army destroyed, 450,000 died
1906 Colorado avalanche wipes out town, 60 died
1910 Cascade Mnts. USA, avalanche, 118 died
1915-18 Alps, 80,000 soldiers killed
1932 Hunan, China, hailstones, 200 died
1951 Vals, Switzerland, buried villages, 240 died
1962 Huascaran, Peru, avalanche, 4,000 died
1970 Huascaran, Peru, 18,000 died

In 1930, five German glider pilots had to bale out during a vicious thunderstorm. They fell to earth as ice-covered human hailstones.

On 30 April 1888, hailstones as big as cricket balls fell in Northern India, killing 246 people and 1,600 sheep and goats.

On 18 July 1953, 60,000 ducks were killed by hailstones falling on Alberta, Canada.

The seven great Ice Ages were disastrous for many species of animal which failed to adapt to the freezing conditions. The woolly mammoth, however, was well adapted to cold. It was probably hunted to extinction by human beings. One mammoth was dug from the Siberian ice early this century. Deep-frozen for over 10,000 years, its meat was fresh enough to be eaten by explorers from the Royal Geographical Society.

Fog, smog and bolts from God

LIGHTNING

Disasters caused by lightning tend to be small scale. The focus of a lightning bolt is not much more than a single human being and its effect is limited unless it starts a fire. Lightning may travel at 100,000 miles per second on its journey between the clouds and the Earth.

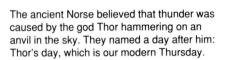

The ancient Norse believed that thunder was caused by the god Thor hammering on an anvil in the sky. They named a day after him: Thor's day, which is our modern Thursday.

An American soldier was welded into his sleeping bag when lightning struck the zip in 1943.

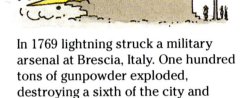

In 1769 lightning struck a military arsenal at Brescia, Italy. One hundred tons of gunpowder exploded, destroying a sixth of the city and wiping out three hundred inhabitants.

Between 1799 and 1815 lightning damaged 150 ships of the Royal Navy with 70 seamen killed and 130 seriously wounded.

What to do if you're caught in a thunderstorm

If you're out in an open space such as a moorland, lie down under a plastic mac.

Don't stand under a tree - trees attract lightning.

A car's metal shell protects its passengers from lightning.

METEORITES

Like lightning, the damage done by meteorites is limited to a small area, unless they are very large or they start a fire.

Most meteorites are smaller than a grain of sand. But one weighing perhaps 70,000 tonnes hit Arizona about 50,000 years ago, leaving a huge crater still visible today.

A meteor which fell on China in 616 BC killed 10 men and broke several chariots.

On 30 June 1908, an object which may have been part of a comet exploded over Siberia. It destroyed over 8 million trees in an area of 2,000 square miles.

One theory about the extinction of the dinosaurs is that a huge meteorite hit the Earth about 65 million years ago raising dust clouds which blotted out the Sun. This made the weather too cold for dinosaur eggs to hatch properly.

SMOG AND FOG

Smog is caused by the effects of industrial pollution and vehicle exhausts on naturally occurring fog. It's quite a recent phenomenon. Fog has always caused problems for people.

In December 1952, 4,000 Londoners died of breathing problems during a coal-fire smog called a 'pea-souper' which lasted 5 days. This prompted the government to bring in the Clean Air Act which made London a smokeless zone.

Before radar was invented, fog caused great problems at sea. In 1914, the liner *Empress of Ireland* collided in dense fog with a coal ship off the Canadian coast. Many of the passengers were asleep at the time. The liner sank in just 15 minutes, carrying 1,012 souls to their panic-stricken deaths.

FAMINE

Ancient Man lived by hunting animals and gathering wild plants to eat. People moved on when the local food supplies ran out. When farming was developed about 8000 BC, people began to live in houses and the size of populations increased. It was then much harder to move away if war or natural disaster struck. Reliance on one or two main crops also increased the risk of famine. If the main crop failed there was little to eat in its stead. Crop failure regularly brought famine to Egypt and other early civilizations. The earliest written reference to a famine is in an Egyptian document of around 3500 BC. Together with war, famine remains the major cause of disaster to this day.

Major famine disasters

3500 BC	Egypt, first recorded famine
436 BC	Rome, famine in the city
1235	London, bark eaten, 20,000 died
1333-37	China, Black Death, famine, 6 million died
1769	France, thousands died
1769-70	India, 13 million died
1790-92	India, 'Skull Famine', millions died
1800-50	China, four major famines, 45 million died
1846-47	Ireland, potato blight, 1,029,552 died
1932-34	USSR, collective farming failed, 5 million died
1967-70	Nigeria, social unrest and crop failure, one million died
1969-74	Sahel Desert, Africa, drought, 1 million died
1984-85	Ethiopia, drought and war, 5 million died

The Irish relied heavily on potatoes in the early nineteenth century. In 1845, a fungus disease called blight destroyed the crop, causing widespread famine during 1846-48. Over a million people died, and a million more emigrated to America.

Potato riot

The 1769 crop failure in France caused famine which wiped out one in twenty of the peasants, and helped set the scene for the later French Revolution.

In 1235, famine caused 20,000 deaths in London. People were reduced to eating grass and the bark of trees.

Pests

Locusts regularly caused famines in ancient Egypt.

Grasshoppers plagued the USA in the 1930s and '40s.

The rice crops of Asia are regularly attacked by Java sparrows.

African weaver birds sometimes form huge flocks up to 20 million strong which devastate crops.

Billions of French Guianian termites ate all that country's crops in the 1940s.

Sixty million mice destroyed crops in Bihar, India in 1899.

Up to 4 million Chinese starved to death between 1333 and 1337. The plague which then attacked the weakened, starving people spread by ship and overland caravans to the rest of the world. This plague was the Black Death.

Drought and famine affected Sudan, Ethiopia and Somalia in the 1960s, '70s and '80s. The deaths of perhaps 5 million Ethiopians in 1984-85 led to the formation of popular charitable efforts such as Band Aid, Live Aid and Comic Relief.

Famine has been recorded in India since around AD 900. The great famine of 1790-1792 was called the 'Doji Bara', or 'skull-famine', because the dead were too numerous to be buried. Only twenty years earlier, in 1769-1770, up to ten million died during a drought in Bihar.

Remedies for Spanish flu

Get very drunk.
Smear hot bacon fat on your neck and chest.
Take a very cold bath.
Take a very hot bath.

The influenza virus produces a new strain every few years. Once in a while a new strain turns out to be a killer. So it was with Spanish flu, 1918-1919. World-wide, 20 million people died in just 120 days. Many different methods of avoiding infection were attempted.

PLAGUE

A disease which is always present in a population is called an endemic disease. Typhoid and cholera are endemic in poor countries without fresh water supplies. The young, the old and the weak are usually the most affected. But sometimes a specially dangerous disease threatens the lives of entire populations. Such diseases are called epidemics. The old word for an epidemic is a plague.

For 12 years from 1338 the Black Death struck Europe and Asia. Victims shivered and sweated, then huge black blobs appeared on their skin and they died in convulsive agony. The plague was carried by infected rats which flourished in the crowded dirty cities of that time. Some infected refugees from the cities were killed by frightened villagers, because they showed symptoms of the plague, such as sneezing. World-wide, 75 million died of the plague.

According to the Book of Exodus in the Bible a plague of boils struck the people and animals of Egypt around 1250 BC.

Leprosy was brought from the Middle East to Europe by the crusaders in the eleventh century. Leprosy was a major killer in the Middle Ages. To warn healthy people that they had the disease, lepers had to wear special clothes and signal their approach with a clapper or bell.

Major Plague disasters	
1250 BC	Egypt, Exodus plagues
1348-1666	Black Death, 25 million world-wide
1520	Mexico, smallpox introduced by Spaniards, 3 million dead
1831	Europe, cholera, 900,000 died
1851-55	Britain, TB, 250,000 died
1904-5	Bengal, plague, 1,500,000 died
1917-21	USSR, typhus, 3 million died
1918-19	Spanish flu, 25 million died world-wide
1960-62	Ethiopia, yellow fever, 20,000 died
1950 on	AIDS, 10 million died world-wide

From 1500, smallpox swept through Europe killing millions. Between 1700 and 1800, sixty million Europeans died of this disease. It was finally eradicated in 1977.

Malaria is spread by mosquitoes. It still kills up to two million people every year. Now largely confined to the tropics, it was once common in Europe.

Yellow fever is another disease which is carried by mosquitoes. Death results from liver or heart failure. Between 1700 and 1900 huge epidemics spread from the tropics into America and Europe. It continues to strike. Between 1960 and 1962 an epidemic killed 20,000 Ethiopians.

White blood cell being attacked by Human Immuno-deficiencey Virus (shown here as purple spheres).

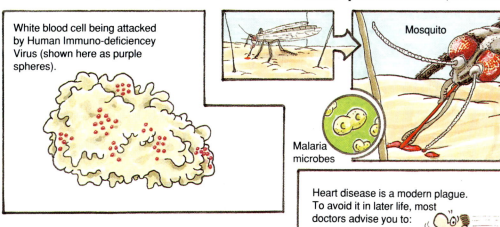

Mosquito

Malaria microbes

Acquired Immune Deficiency Syndrome (AIDS) is thought to have been endemic in Central Africa for centuries and may have been passed to humans by the bites of Green Monkeys. However, it only emerged as an international killer in the 1950s. It has now spread around the world, mostly by sexual contact. There are about 10 million cases now and by the year 2000 this may have risen to 40 million.

Heart disease is a modern plague. To avoid it in later life, most doctors advise you to:

eat less fat

not smoke

take regular exercise

How to survive a nuclear attack

1. Live a long way from potential targets such as cities.

2. Build a strong underground shelter. Fill it with stores.

3. Radioactivity should fall to fairly safe levels after about 60 years.

WAR

The use of force to resolve conflicts between groups of people is probably as old as the human race itself. It has been estimated that there have been only 300 years when no wars were recorded since written history began about 5,000 years ago. War has probably claimed more victims than any other type of disaster, especially since famine, fire and plague often follow in its wake.

During the Battle of Crécy, 1346, English bowman released up to 60,000 arrows a minute at the advancing French cavalry. One and a half thousand French knights were killed.

Approximately three-quarters of the male population of Britain died or were enslaved during the Roman Conquest, AD 43-84.

When the French army was passing through Poland on its way to Moscow in July 1812, 80,000 men died of, or were sick with, typhus.

Major war disasters
Since 1500 BC there have been at least 378 named wars. The estimated number of military deaths alone is more than 45 million.

The highest death toll caused by a single bomb occurred on 6th August 1945, when an atom bomb was dropped on Hiroshima, Japan, killing 140,000 people.

'Little Boy', the first atomic bomb

Brave but crazy

Lord Cardigan led the Charge of the Light Brigade in 1854 during the Crimean War. Six hundred and seven English cavalrymen armed only with swords charged Russian artillery positions. Four hundred and nine were killed. Lord Cardigan rode right through the enemy lines and back again without noticing the disaster. The buttoned woolly garment called a cardigan is named after him.

'General' George A. Custer led a force of 212 men against a much greater force of Sioux braves at Little Big Horn in June 1876. His entire force was killed.

Pyrrhus, the Greek commander at the Battle of Beneventum in 275 BC, was beaten by the Roman forces when one of his military elephants ran amuck and slaughtered many of his own troops.

Military expenditure during World War II is put at $1.5 trillion. This is more than all the other wars in history put together.

General Robert E. Lee thought his Confederate troops were invincible. After three days of suicidal attacks against fortified Union lines at Gettysburg, 1865, 7,500 of his men had died.

Different cultures have used some strange currency...

Native Americans: necklaces of shells called wampum.

Ancient Irish: gold rings.

Chinese: symbolic bronze knives.

Aztecs: copper axes.

Yap Islanders (Pacific): huge carved stones weighing up to half a ton.

FINANCIAL FOUL-UPS

Before money was invented, people traded by bartering. But this was often inconvenient. Travelling traders had to carry all their heavy goods with them. Metal money was first used about 600 BC by the Lydians of Asia Minor (now Turkey). Small pieces of gold or silver were stamped with a design or a king's head to show they contained a particular weight of precious metal. These 'coins' could then be exchanged for goods of an equal value.

Paper money was first used instead of metal coins in China during the reign of Kublai Khan (1215-1294). But paper money, cheques and share certificates only have value as long as people believe that these pieces of paper represent real wealth, because the paper they are written on has no value in itself. The system works as long as people believe in it. Sometimes for a variety of reasons, people stop believing. When that happens there is a financial crisis.

After losing the First World War, Germany was forced to pay reserves of gold to the victors. In the meantime the German banks continued to print paper money. But paper money is really only a promise to pay. If a government is bankrupt, its paper money becomes worthless. If the government has no other form of wealth, such as gold, to back up its paper money, the paper money eventually becomes worthless. Confidence in the German mark collapsed. In 1914, one US dollar was worth four marks. By 1924, it was worth four TRILLION marks. People took wages home in wheelbarrows. Inflation was so rapid that a cup of coffee could double in price between sips. Thousands of people faced starvation.

Children played in the streets with worthless banknotes.

In 1929 a few business failures led to unease and then to wholesale panic as other share prices fell on the Wall Street Stock Exchange in the USA. People queued overnight to retrieve money from their bank accounts. Banks ran out of money - 11,000 of them went bankrupt by 1933. Ruined bankers and business men committed suicide by jumping into rivers or out of tall buildings. The Wall Street Crash led to the Great Depression of the 1930s when there was massive unemployment in America and Europe.

Towards the end of the Roman Empire the government in Rome became desperate for money to pay its armies and public servants. More and more coins were produced. This caused massive inflation which weakened the Roman Empire still further.

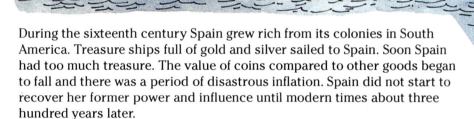

During the sixteenth century Spain grew rich from its colonies in South America. Treasure ships full of gold and silver sailed to Spain. Soon Spain had too much treasure. The value of coins compared to other goods began to fall and there was a period of disastrous inflation. Spain did not start to recover her former power and influence until modern times about three hundred years later.

In England in 1720 the South Sea Company which traded with South America appeared to be hugely profitable. There was a greedy scramble to buy shares in the company. Millions of pounds changed hands and the price of shares reached ridiculous heights. But buyers were being deceived by the company directors and the real value of the shares was far less. When no profits appeared, panic selling led to the collapse of these and other overpriced shares. Britain's entire economy was almost destroyed as the 'South Sea Bubble' burst.

In 1634 one Dutch merchant traded these items for a single rare tulip bulb:
two lasts of wheat
four lasts of rye
four fat oxen
eight fat swine
twelve fat sheep
two hogsheads of wine
four tuns of beer
two tuns of butter
a thousand pounds of cheese
a complete bed
a suit of clothes
a silver drinking-cup

In the 1630s Dutch tulips became very valuable. The Dutch economy became dependent on tulips. When the price of tulips collapsed there was a major financial disaster in Holland with mass poverty and suicides.

INDUSTRIAL DISASTERS

The Industrial Age is reckoned to have started in England around 1750 when steam and steel technology was first developed. Since that time industrial accidents have become more deadly as industry has used ever more dangerous chemicals and ever larger amounts of energy.

Many industrial accidents start with explosions. These kill directly or cause leaks of poisonous chemicals. They can kill or injure people far away from the source of the accident. The effects of accidents in nuclear power plants have been felt thousands of miles away.

Although industrial disasters hit the headlines, more death and injury is caused by the small-scale accidents which happen every day.
Workers fall into vats of beer in breweries, composers go deaf, printers fall into printing presses...

In 1986, a nuclear reactor exploded at the Chernobyl power station in the Ukraine. A toxic cloud of radioactive gas spread out over Europe. Eight thousand may have died from radiation sickness. This was the world's worst nuclear accident.

On 7 December 1917 the *Mont Blanc* was rammed by another ship in the harbour of Halifax, Nova Scotia. She was carrying explosives. The resulting blast killed 2,000 people.

In 1929, 1,000 people are thought to have died when a secret germ warfare factory blew up at Sverdlovsk in the former USSR. Deadly anthrax germs were spread over a large area.

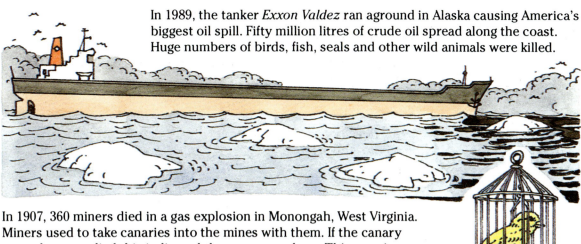

In 1989, the tanker *Exxon Valdez* ran aground in Alaska causing America's biggest oil spill. Fifty million litres of crude oil spread along the coast. Huge numbers of birds, fish, seals and other wild animals were killed.

In 1907, 360 miners died in a gas explosion in Monongah, West Virginia. Miners used to take canaries into the mines with them. If the canary grew sleepy or died this indicated the presence of gas. This warning system was not entirely foolproof.

In 1984 at Bhopal, India, a poisonous gas leaked from a storage tank at a factory which make batteries. At least 2,500 local people are recorded as dying from the poisonous, choking fumes. At least 500,000 more were injured but lived to file damage claims against the American factory owners, Union Carbide.

In the 1950s, a chemical plant at Minamata, Japan, emptied poisonous mercury compounds into the sea. At least 150 of the local population soon died from eating contaminated fish. Others are still suffering from brain damage.

Major industrial disasters
1866 Oaks colliery, England, explosions, 361 died
1907 Monongah Mine, West Virginia, explosion 360 died
1913 Senghenydd Colliery, Wales, explosion 439 died
1917 Halifax, Nova Scotia, explosion on a ship, 2,000 died
1947 Texas City Harbour, fire spreading to 50 oil tankers, 800 died
1953-93 Minamata, Japan, mercury leak, 300 died to date
1966 Aberfan, Wales, coal tip slide, 116 children died
1967 *Torrey Canyon*, oil tanker spillage, massive ecological damage to UK coast.
1976 Seveso Italy, chemical factory explosion, massive ecological damage
1979 Sverdlovsk, USSR, anthrax germ leak, 1000 died
1979 *Aegean Captain* and *Atlantic Empress*, two-tanker collision, world's biggest oilspill, 27 died
1984 Bhopal, India, chemical factory leak, 2,500 died
1986 Chernobyl, Ukraine, nuclear power explosion, 8,000 died
1989 Alaska, *Exxon Valdez* oil tanker spillage, massive ecological damage to coast

Flames from the 1944 Cleveland Ohio gas explosion rose 2,800 feet into the air. Pigeons fell to ground having been fully roasted in mid-air.

The safest place to sit

On the deck of a ship.

At the back of a train.

In the back passenger seat of a car.

At the back of an aeroplane.

TRANSPORT

One of the earliest descriptions of an accident involving transport is in the Old Testament. When pursuing the Israelites in their flight from Egypt, Pharaoh's chariots sank in the Red Sea.

But it was when transport became motorised that more transport accidents happened. The first, steam-driven, automobile crashed on its first run in 1769. Ships and trains made travel available to hundreds and sometimes thousands of people at a time.

The giant airships were filled with highly inflammable hydrogen gas. On 6 May 1937, the German airship liner *Hindenberg* burst into flames when landing in New Jersey. Static electrical sparks from a mooring mast had started the fire. Miraculously, out of 97 on board, only 33 died. This was the last of a number of fatal fires involving hydrogen airships.

The highest death toll in a single plane accident occurred in 1977 when two planes collided on the runway of Tenerife airport. Five hundred and eighty-three people died.

Major air disasters
1913 *LZ-18* German airship, first major air disaster, 28 died
1930 British R101 airship, explosion, 48 died
1937 *Hindenburg*, German airship, fire, 33 died
1974 Forest near Paris, Turkish airlines crash, 344 died
1977 Tenerife airport, runway collision, 583 died
1985 Mount Osutaka, Japan airline crash, 520 died
1988 Lockerbie, Pan Am terrorist bomb, 270 died
1989 Off Ireland, Air India terrorist bomb, 329 died

Major train disasters
1864 Shohola, Pennsylvania, head-on collision, 148 died
1879 Tay Bridge collapsed, Scotland, 75 died
1915 Troop train in collision with two other trains, Scotland, 227 died
1917 Troop train brake failure, Modane, France, 543 died
1944 Train collision, Salerno, Italy, 526 died
1981 Bridge collapsed, Bihar, India, 800 died
1989 Gas pipeline explosion, two trains passing, Siberia, 500 died

The first recorded death from a train accident occurred at the opening ceremony of the Liverpool to London line in 1830. An over-excited MP, William Huskisson, fell in front of *The Rocket.* His leg was severed.

In one of the world's worst train disasters, 543 soldiers died when the brakes failed on a troop train going down hill in France in 1917. It crashed on a bend having reached a speed of 100 mph.

The world's worst road disaster happened in the Salang Tunnel linking the USSR and Afghanistan in 1982. Two military convoys were involved. Possibly 2,000 people died from fumes and other injuries.

People were frightened by the speed and power of the first motor cars. In some countries the law insisted that a man with a red flag walk in front of every car.

On 7th May 1915, the US luxury liner *Lusitania* was sunk by a German U-boat. 1,198 lives were lost. Americans were outraged by this attack and in 1917 joined in the First World War against the Germans.

Thinking that the liner *Titanic* was unsinkable, some passengers held a snowball fight on deck with pieces of ice after their ship had collided with an iceberg. One thousand five hundred and three of the two thousand two hundred and seven passengers and crew perished when the *Titanic* sank.

Major ship disasters
1865 Mississippi river, *Sultana* steamer overloaded, 1,547 died
1849 Manchuria, Chinese troopship exploded, 6,000 died
1904 East River, New York, *General Slocum* ferry boat caught fire, 1,021 died
1912 North Atlantic, *Titanic* collides with iceberg, 1,503 died
1915 *Lusitania*, sunk by German submarine, 1,198 died
1954 Japan, *Taya Maru* ferry sunk by typhoon, over 1,000 died

The safest place on Earth
It is estimated that Sunnynook, Canada is the safest place on Earth. It is far from any fault line so there is no danger of earthquake or volcano. Canada is not engaged in any wars. There is no danger of flooding, not much traffic so little danger of accidents, and there are modern health services to cope with disease. There's plenty of food so there is no danger of starvation. Central Canada does not suffer from hurricanes. The only danger is snow - and they're well prepared.

RESCUE AND PREVENTION

The damage caused by natural disasters can be reduced if people have some warning that a disaster is about to happen. These days there are various scientific methods of predicting natural disasters.

Man-made disasters should be more preventable than natural disasters, but regulations and safety devices often fail, and there is always the possibility of human error.

Once a disaster has happened, the work of rescue can stretch the resources of a country to the limit. Most countries now have rescue services which are kept in a state of readiness in case a disaster should occur. Even so the problems caused by a major disaster can be overwhelming.

Scientists have had some success in predicting earthquakes and volcanic eruptions. Close study over many years allowed scientists to predict the eruption of Mount St Helens, USA, in 1980.

Lighthouses have saved many sailors from shipwreck. The 130 metre Pharos lighthouse in Egypt was built in 200 BC and was one of the Seven Wonders of the Ancient World. It was destroyed by an earthquake on July 21, AD 365.

The 'black box' flight recorder which rescuers search for after air crashes is usually bright orange so it can be seen easily.

Since the 1970s, hurricanes have been tracked by weather satellites so an early warning can be given about their paths. The practice of naming hurricanes was started by the Australian Clarence Wragg in the nineteenth century, who called them after people he didn't like.

Throughout the centuries, people have tried to stop hail damaging crops. The Greeks sacrificed animals and Italian peasants rang bells and hung out lucky charms.

Around 1900, European farmers tried firing blank charges from a 'hail cannon' to shatter hailstones before they fell.

Rescue vehicles

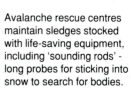

Fleets of ambulances are needed to evacuate victims.

Helicopters are useful after most disasters.

Planes have been used to bomb lava flows in order to divert the course of lava away from towns.

In Russia, planes drop cement powder onto clouds to precipitate rain and thus avoid both droughts and storms.

The first fire engines were horse drawn vehicles owned by private insurance companies.

In Southern France and Canada, planes scoop water from the sea or the lakes to fight forest fires.

Mobile cranes and bulldozers are often needed to remove fallen masonry from the victims of earthquakes or explosions.

Fire-ships pump water directly from bodies of open water.

The hulls of lifeboats were once filled with ping-pong balls to reduce the danger of sinking.

Avalanche rescue centres maintain sledges stocked with life-saving equipment, including 'sounding rods' - long probes for sticking into snow to search for bodies.

FUTURE DISASTERS

In the past, man-made disasters have been much less destructive than natural disasters, but in the future this may change. Environmental damage due to human activity, such as global warming, could result in disasters on a scale never seen before. And in the meantime, natural disasters like volcanoes, hurricanes and earthquakes will continue to happen. A fairly horrible history could turn into a very horrible future.

Ice Ages have occurred regularly for the last seven million years. The last one ended 10,000 years ago. The next one may be on its way.

The Norse believed that there would be three years of perpetual winter before Ragnarok, or Doomsday.

An estimated 100 billion meteorites strike the Earth's atmosphere every day. Most of them are small and burn up before hitting the surface. But a giant meteorite may have caused the extinction of the dinosaurs. Another giant may hit at any time.

Overpopulation is a present day disaster. The rate of increase in the world's population makes it likely that famines and wars will be even more destructive in the future.

Careless use of agricultural genetic engineering may upset the world's ecological balance.

Modern weapons systems are immensely powerful. There are more than enough nuclear weapons in the world to destroy all human life.

Deadly new microbes may escape from laboratories causing epidemics far worse than the plague or AIDS.

The temperature of the Earth's atmosphere may rise due to our use of fossil fuels. The ice caps could melt, causing sea levels to rise. Most of the world's major cities are built near the sea.

One disaster is certain to happen. In about 10 billion years the Sun will die. If the human race survives that long, it will have done very well indeed!

THE HUMAN MACHINE

Your body is an amazing machine. It has hundreds of muscles and bones, thousands of kilometres of tubes, millions of nerves and billions of cells. All this is hidden beneath your skin. Unless we know how things work we can't fix them when they go wrong. People used to be very ignorant about how bodies worked. This led to many strange and dangerous treatments. The first real attempts to discover how the body works were made by the ancient Greeks. Since the European Renaissance, and especially in the last three hundred years, medical research has accelerated.

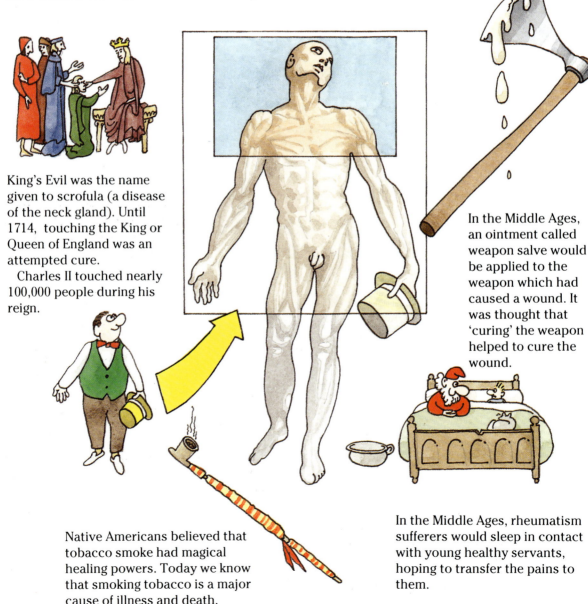

King's Evil was the name given to scrofula (a disease of the neck gland). Until 1714, touching the King or Queen of England was an attempted cure.
Charles II touched nearly 100,000 people during his reign.

In the Middle Ages, an ointment called weapon salve would be applied to the weapon which had caused a wound. It was thought that 'curing' the weapon helped to cure the wound.

Native Americans believed that tobacco smoke had magical healing powers. Today we know that smoking tobacco is a major cause of illness and death.

In the Middle Ages, rheumatism sufferers would sleep in contact with young healthy servants, hoping to transfer the pains to them.

Until AD 161 it was thought that arteries carried air. In that year Galen, a Greek doctor, discovered that they carry blood. It was forbidden to dissect, or cut up, human bodies until the sixteenth century, so Galen used to cut up apes and pigs. He assumed human bodies worked in the same way as the animals he dissected. His theories formed the basis of medical opinion for 1,500 years.

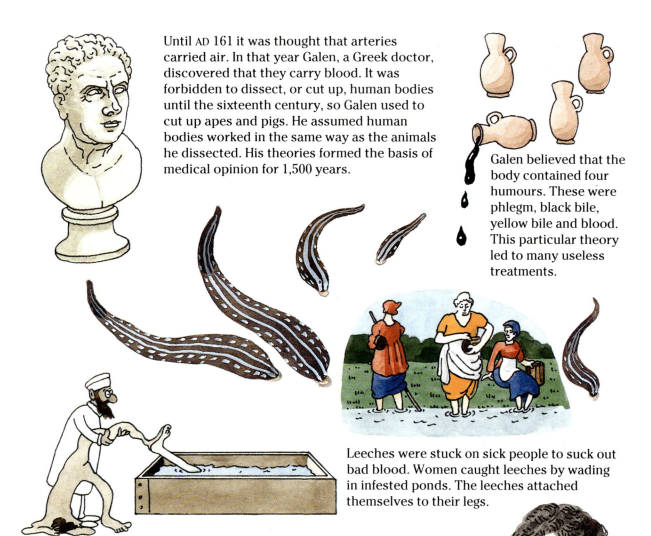

Galen believed that the body contained four humours. These were phlegm, black bile, yellow bile and blood. This particular theory led to many useless treatments.

Leeches were stuck on sick people to suck out bad blood. Women caught leeches by wading in infested ponds. The leeches attached themselves to their legs.

All major religions and civilisations at one time or another have banned dissection of the human body. However, ancient Hindus were allowed to soak bodies in water and then peel back the skin so that they could look inside and study them.

Andreas Vesalius, an Italian doctor, wrote the first scientific text on the human body in 1543. He was condemned to death by the Catholic Church, but was saved by the Holy Roman Emperor.

Throughout the Middle Ages, the examination of urine was the main way of diagnosing disease. This was despite the fact that doctors didn't know what they were looking for.

It seems that cleanliness was valued by some ancient civilisations. The remains of public baths 4,500 years old have been found in Pakistan, Iraq and Egypt.

LIVING CONDITIONS

The average lifespan of Stone Age people was less than eighteen years. The main causes of death were disease and violence.

Improvements in farming methods, sanitation, housing and medicine have helped people to live longer and longer, but many of the major diseases of history have been made worse by the crowded living conditions of town life. The importance of cleanliness was not properly understood until the nineteenth century.

By 1900, city dwellers in Europe and the USA could expect to live until fifty. Slum housing, bad water and air pollution meant that people still died younger than today.

In the USA today, both men and women can expect to live to at least seventy. The reason that people live so much longer nowadays is due far more to public health measures and a good diet than to the wonders of modern medicine.

Castles had toilets built into the walls. Toilet waste fell outside the castle.

A toilet built over the River Thames collapsed while occupied. In the Middle Ages, toilets often emptied directly into rivers.

A pomander is a perfumed ball which some people carried to ward off infection and counteract bad smells.

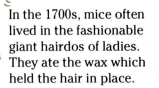

In the 1700s, mice often lived in the fashionable giant hairdos of ladies. They ate the wax which held the hair in place.

Medieval people often used the floor as a toilet. Layers of reeds or rushes were spread on top occasionally. When mixed with clay, the waste made saltpetre, an ingredient of gunpowder. A saltpetre law forbade the paving of floors in England until 1634.

Norman castles were dirty places, but they sometimes had large bathrooms where families could bathe together.

Medieval towns had open-air bath houses called stews. Men and women bathed together.

Puritans didn't approve of bathing. They felt it weakened the body.

In many houses, cellars were used as cess pits, which were shovelled out occasionally into a cart. Water contaminated by cess pits spread typhoid and cholera.

Slipper baths, which took their name from their shape, hid the bather from servants who poured in water. They were popular in nineteenth century America, as can be seen from western movies.

Tuberculosis was spread by spitting and coughing. Spittoons were commonplace in the nineteenth century. These were containers in public places for spitting into.

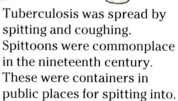

Two thousand five hundred tonnes of lead from car exhausts are released into the atmosphere every year. Lead limits brain growth in children.

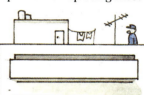

Until the smog laws of 1962, a photochemical smog covered the city of Los Angeles for 212 days of the year.

Modern living conditions can also cause disease. Large office buildings with windows which can't be opened can be breeding grounds for diseases.

In 350 BC, the Romans built the first aqueduct to bring water to Rome. Roman cities had piped clean water and sewers. It took modern European cities until 1800 to match their standards.

YOU ARE WHAT YOU EAT

Variety in the food we eat is important to health. The Romans ate a huge range of foods. Today, the Chinese eat a wider variety of food than any other peoples. Delicacies include snake, fried fish stomachs and chickens' feet.

For most of history human beings have not been farmers, they have been hunter-gatherers. The human body is designed to work best on the sort of food which might be eaten by a hunter-gatherer, such as fresh fruit and nuts with a small amount of meat. Farming is a relatively recent invention, and modern factory food is even more recent.

People only started farming in Europe about 4,000 years ago and modern factory food wasn't produced until 40 years ago. Modern foods are the cause of much ill health; however, the food eaten in the West is much healthier than it has been for several hundred years.

Diatetics is the study of food. It's a very old science. A guide to good eating was written 3,500 years ago in Egypt.

The ancient Greeks thought that food was made of the four elements: earth, air, fire and water. Hot, spicy food was fire. Moist food was water. Dry food was earth. Cool, light food was air.

Children do not grow properly if they eat poor food. Until recently, the Japanese and poorer people in the West were very short because of a bad diet in childhood.

Margarine was one of the first factory foods. Originally it was made of beef fat, milk and minced cow's udders.

Baked dormouse was considered a delicacy by rich Romans.

In the nineteenth century, bread often contained bone dust or chalk, wood shavings and a poisonous chemical called alum to make it look whiter. Mixing bad products with food is called adulteration.

Henry VIII of England suffered from scurvy and other diseases, because he ate hardly anything but meat. Scurvy is a disease caused by not eating enough fresh vegetables.

In the 1800s, an Italian cheese manufacturer sold Parmesan cheese which was mainly made of grated umbrella handles.

COUGHS AND SNEEZES

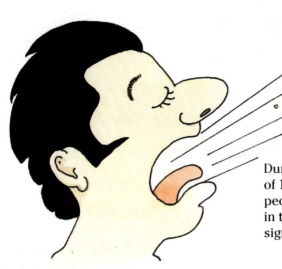

People used to think that disease was caused by evil influences called miasmas. Miasmas were found in things such as wood, soil, water or animals.

During the Spanish flu epidemic of 1918-19, which killed more people than all the soldiers killed in the First World War, huge signs in New York announced:

IT IS UNLAWFUL TO COUGH OR SNEEZE

$500 FINE

Infectious diseases are passed from one person to another. They are caused by tiny life forms called germs.

A sneeze bursts from the nose at 100 mph. It blasts as many as 100,000 drops of germ-rich mucus up to a distance of 2.5 metres away. If the sneezer has a disease, the germs in any of these drops may spread that disease.

The idea that tiny creatures might cause disease was discussed in a Roman encyclopaedia 2,000 years ago, but it could not be proved because germs are far too tiny to see with the naked eye. Zacharias Janssen is thought to have invented the microscope in 1590. By 1677, microscopes had become powerful enough for another Dutchman, Anton Van Leeuwenhoek, to discover single-celled 'animalcules', or germs.

Typhus was known as gaol fever, where it killed thousands. It was caused by a body louse which could jump from one prisoner to another in crowded prison conditions. This disease also wiped out most of Napoleon's Grande Armée in 1812.

In America, 60 million schooldays are lost each year because of the common cold.

Smallpox virus

Some very small germs called viruses cause diseases. They are so small that they cannot be seen under a standard microscope. Mumps, measles, chicken pox, influenza and the common cold are all caused by viruses.

Louis Pasteur

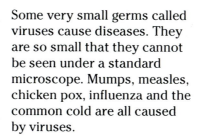
Influenza was recorded in ancient Rome in 412 BC.

Louis Pasteur (1822-95) showed experimentally that infectious diseases are caused by germs. We still use 'pasteurisation', the gentle heating of drinks and foodstuffs, to help prevent infections.

Humans can catch some diseases from animals such as rabies from dogs and fevers from parrots and rabbits.

So many people were killed by cholera in Lower Bengal that the disease was worshipped as the Goddess Cholera.

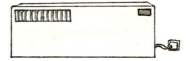

Legionnaires disease was discovered in 1976. It is caused by bacteria that like to live in air conditioning systems in buildings.

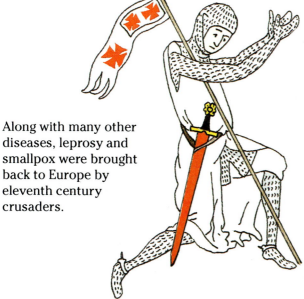

Along with many other diseases, leprosy and smallpox were brought back to Europe by eleventh century crusaders.

European colonists spread many infectious diseases around the world. Millions of Native Americans died of smallpox and measles which were unknown in ancient America before the settlers arrived.

PLAGUE

This mask was worn by doctors visiting plague victims. It is made of leather with glass eyes and a long nose stuffed with perfume.

From time to time a disease will spread rapidly from one person to the next like a forest fire. Sometimes millions of people die. A disease on this scale is called a plague. The word was first used by Galen, the famous Greek doctor, in the second century AD. One of the most devastating tragedies ever was the bubonic plague, otherwise known as the Black Death. It spread from China in the 1330s and killed around 75 million people, 25 million of them in Europe. So many people died that eventually the dead were left to rot where they fell. Bubonic plague continued to haunt Europe for the next two hundred years.

Today, plagues are more often called epidemics. The worst epidemic of modern times was the Spanish flu of 1918-19. It killed 21,600,000 people in 120 days.

During the Black Death in fourteenth century Byzantium, the dead were piled in the towers of the city walls. The stench was horrible.

In 1347, the Mongol army catapulted plague victims into the besieged city of Caffa to infect the inhabitants.

Many Europeans believed that Jews caused the plague by poisoning wells. In Mainz, Germany, 12,000 Jews were burned because of this.

How to tell if you have caught the plague

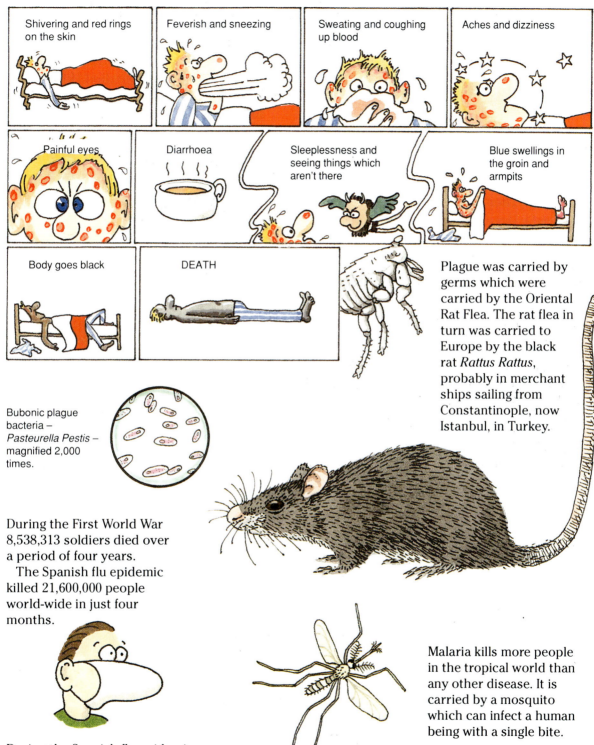

Plague was carried by germs which were carried by the Oriental Rat Flea. The rat flea in turn was carried to Europe by the black rat *Rattus Rattus*, probably in merchant ships sailing from Constantinople, now Istanbul, in Turkey.

Bubonic plague bacteria – *Pasteurella Pestis* – magnified 2,000 times.

During the First World War 8,538,313 soldiers died over a period of four years.

The Spanish flu epidemic killed 21,600,000 people world-wide in just four months.

During the Spanish flu epidemic, the people of San Francisco could be jailed for not wearing white cotton face masks on the street.

Malaria kills more people in the tropical world than any other disease. It is carried by a mosquito which can infect a human being with a single bite.

Today, a disease called AIDS is spreading rapidly. AIDS is turning into a modern epidemic.

DOCTORS AND MEDICINE MEN

Early healers were often magicians or priests. Magical treatments are normal among primitive tribes even today.

Professional doctors are as old as civilisation. The ancient Chinese practised acupuncture 6,000 years ago. Ancient Hindu doctors wrote down their theories in the *Rig Veda* 3,500 years ago. And the ancient Egyptians had doctors, although they were reluctant to treat patients, because if the patient died the doctor was executed.

Western medicine started with the ancient Greeks. Modern doctors still swear the 'Hippocratic oath', named after a Greek doctor called Hippocrates who was born in 460 BC. This oath pledges doctors to maintain the well-being of their patients above all things. Since ancient Egyptian times, doctors have tried to control who can and who can't treat patients. Today, people without medical training are not allowed to call themselves doctors of medicine. This protects the public from ignorant, unqualified doctors.

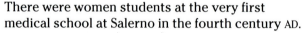

There were women students at the very first medical school at Salerno in the fourth century AD.

Midwives help women give birth to babies. Male midwives were forbidden to look at their female patients under the bed clothes. So they believed a lady in Godalming when she claimed to have given birth to fifteen rabbits in 1726.

Eye doctor   Mouth doctor   Ear doctor   Foot doctor

Asclepius was the Greek god of healing.

Specialists are nothing new. In ancient Egypt, priest doctors specialised in just one part of the body.

Doctors have been called many rude names in the past such as Sawbones, Leech, Charlatan and Quack. Quack doctors used to tour the Wild West. The name 'quack' comes from the sound they made when shouting to sell their cures. They worked from wagons so that they could make a quick escape if they were discovered to be frauds. Dr Perkins was a famous American quack. His electro-magnetic rods were supposed to draw diseases from the body.

Native American priest doctors, sometimes called Medicine Men, wore a necklace called a soul catcher. They believed that sick people had lost their souls and the necklace helped to capture the soul and return it to the body.

Among the Cree tribe of Native Americans, medicine women cured the sick. Some African tribes have medicine women to this day.

In some developing countries today, men and women are taught basic medical skills so that they can look after poor people in the countryside cheaply. They are nicknamed 'barefoot doctors'.

The Countess of Kent's powder was a quack cure meant to cure the Plague. It contained the feet of large sea crabs, pearls, coral and vipers.

Since the eighteenth century medical schools have turned out more and more doctors each year. Today, there are 465,000 doctors in the USA alone.

TOOLS OF MEDICINE

By using a laser, a modern surgeon can operate inside the body without cutting the skin. If the surgeon wants to look inside a brain he can do so with the huge four-tonne nuclear magnetic resonance scanner.

Today's doctors make use of tools which would have been unimaginable to earlier generations.

But despite the advances in medical technology, some surgical tools have changed very little over the last three thousand years. Knives and saws for cutting flesh and bone are still in use today.

Before the danger of infection was understood, surgeon's saws and knives were often thick with blood and pus from earlier operations.

Stone Age surgeons often cut holes in the skull with a flint chisel, possibly to stop headaches or to let out devils. This operation is called trepanning. Sometimes boiling oil was poured into the wound.

Today, surgical maggots can be used to clean wounds. They eat the dirt round the wound. Simon Stylites, a hermit who lived on top of a pillar, encouraged maggots to live on his rotting body, saying to them, 'Eat what the Lord has provided.'

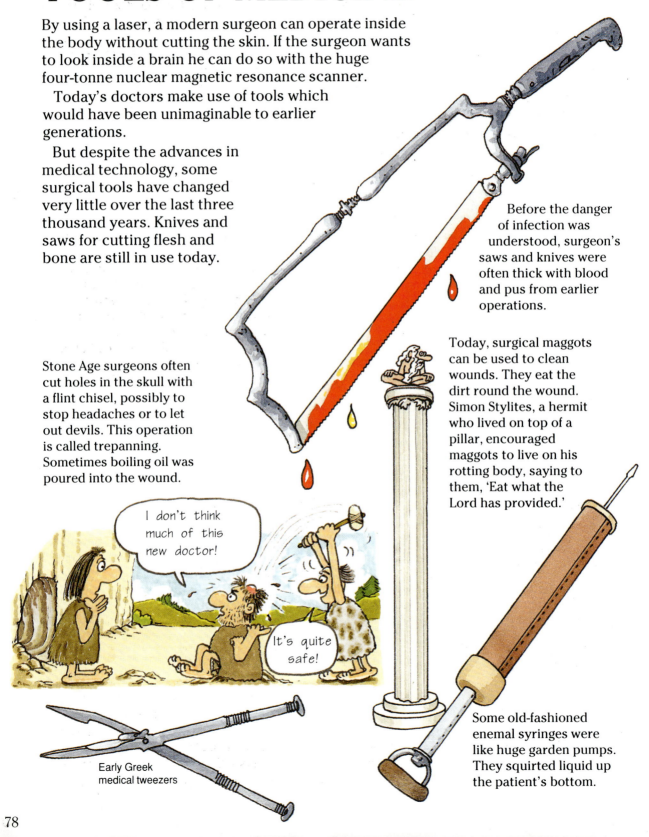

I don't think much of this new doctor!

It's quite safe!

Early Greek medical tweezers

Some old-fashioned enemal syringes were like huge garden pumps. They squirted liquid up the patient's bottom.

The hypodermic syringe was developed after an Irishman called Francis Rynd invented the hollow needle. The first useful metal syringe was invented in 1853 by a Frenchman called Dr Charles Pravaz. The hypodermic syringe may soon be replaced by a new invention called iontophoresis. This allows injecting without puncturing the skin.

Radioactive chemicals can be injected into the blood stream. Radiation detectors follow their course through the body. This technique can be useful for discovering heart and brain defects.

Galileo invented a thermometer in 1593, but it was inaccurate. In the seventeenth century, Robert Boyle made a sealed thermometer which could measure the blood heat of humans.

Stethoscopes are used to listen to the working of the heart and lungs. Early doctors put their ears directly on the patient's chest. In the eighteenth century, René Laennec, a Breton, invented a simple stethoscope made of rolled up paper. Modern stethoscopes were developed in the nineteenth century. Doctors used to keep them under their top hats.

An excess of blood was thought to cause illness. Barber surgeons used a knife, a cup and a piece of string to remove it. The barber's pole symbolises this ancient bloodletting practice.

X-rays were discovered by a German called Wilhelm Roentgen. He used his wife's hand for the first pictures.

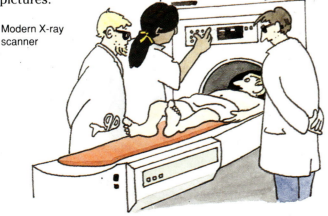

Modern X-ray scanner

Another method of bloodletting was called cupping. The patient's skin was scratched and the scratch was covered by a hot glass cup. A vacuum formed and blood was sucked into the cup.

ILLS AND PILLS

There are 600,000 plant species in the world. Almost 1,000 useful drugs have been found in them, and only 30,000 species have been studied so far. Most plant species are found in the rain forests which are being cut down at an alarming rate. Chinese pharmacists use many plant medicines unknown in the West.

Swallowing live frogs was thought to ease a sore throat. The slime on the frog's back was thought to be soothing.

A cure for headache was to chew the leaves of the white willow tree. There is a drug in the leaves called willow-herb. A similar drug called aspirin is now being made artificially.

Most drugs come from plants. Until the 1900s people normally ate the whole plant, or parts of it. It was not known how to remove active drugs from plants. Drugs and medicines were prepared by apothecaries or pharmacists in their shops and there were very few drug companies.

Today, drugs can be removed from plants and made into medicine. In the USA alone, over one thousand drug companies manufacture these medicines. Around the world huge sums of money are spent on drugs each year.

The foxglove plant was used in many country remedies. William Withering discovered that it contained a drug called digitalis, which is now used to treat heart conditions.

Curare is used by South American Indians on the tips of their poison darts. It is now used as a muscle relaxant before surgical operations.

Ancient Peruvians chewed the bark of the Cinchona tree to treat mosquito bites. The active drug in the bark is called quinine. It has been used to treat malaria in Europe since 1640.

How pills are made

Some medicines are natural plant extracts, but most are made in factories.

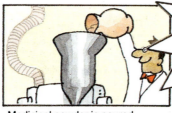
Medicinal powder is poured into a stamping machine.

One in six admissions to hospitals in the USA are due to the side-effects of medicines.

The machine stamps the powder into pill form.

Another machine covers the pills with a protective coating.

The pills then go to the bottling machine.

To stop internal bleeding a bag with a dried toad inside was hung round the neck.

Saliva is a natural medicine. In the wars with ancient Rome, the wives of German warriors used to clean the wounds of their husbands by licking them.

Crushed beetles and pig fat were taken to cure skin rashes.

Alexander Fleming

Penicillin cures many types of infection. It was the first antibiotic to be discovered and is the most useful drug of all time. It comes from a mould which was discovered by accident by Alexander Fleming in 1928.

A fourteenth century cure for the common cold was to boil red onion and mustard together and then stuff the mixture up the sufferer's nose.

Some plants which are commonly consumed today were once thought to be medicines. These include rhubarb, tobacco, tea and coffee.

OPERATIONS

The history of operations is largely one of horrific pain, fear, infection and death. It is less than a hundred years since surgery started to become the fairly safe and painless thing it is today.

Until recently, the only anaesthetics were opium, a drink of alcohol or a blow to the head. There was no knowledge of hygiene, and surgeons would operate in old robes which were soaked in blood and pus from previous operations. Most patients died from shock and pain, from blood loss or from infections.

Joseph Lister (1827-1912) developed a method of spraying the area of an operation with carbolic acid. This greatly reduced infections.

Cobwebs or hot tar were used to stem the flow of blood after an operation. Ambroise Paré (1517-1590), who is known as the father of modern surgery, was a French army doctor who treated wounds with ointment instead of hot tar. Today, wounds are stitched up with surgical thread.

Ether, a form of alcohol, became a common anaesthetic in the nineteenth century. The first anaesthetic machine was an ether inhaler used in Boston, Massachusetts, in 1847.

Chloroform was first tested by a party of doctors in 1847. It became the most popular anaesthetic, and was later used on Queen Victoria.

It was very important to perform operations quickly because of the pain and the loss of blood. In the 1840s Robert Lister held the world record for amputating a leg in just two and half minutes.

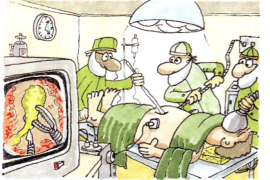

Modern 'keyhole surgery' allows surgeons to operate without cutting big holes. The surgeon operates through small openings made in the skin, using tiny surgical instruments on flexible rods. Optic fibres connected to a visual display unit allow the surgeon to see what's happening inside the body.

Julius Caesar, the first Roman Emperor, was cut from his mother's body at birth in an operation which is now called a Caesarian section.

Nowadays, surgeons and nurses wear very clean clothes. They also wear masks to stop microbes in their breath entering the patient. The first sterile rubber gloves were developed by the American William Halstead.

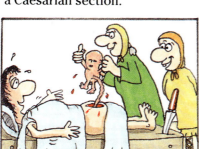

Early anaesthetics included alcoholic drinks, opium and other drugs.

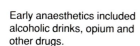

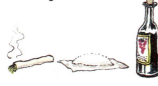

The ancient Chinese knew how to stop pain using tiny spikes called acupuncture needles. The technique is still useful today.

Native American culture refused to recognise that pain existed. Children were taught to withstand pain.

In 1844, an American dentist called Horace Wells used laughing gas to anaesthetise his patients.

ARTIFICIAL PARTS

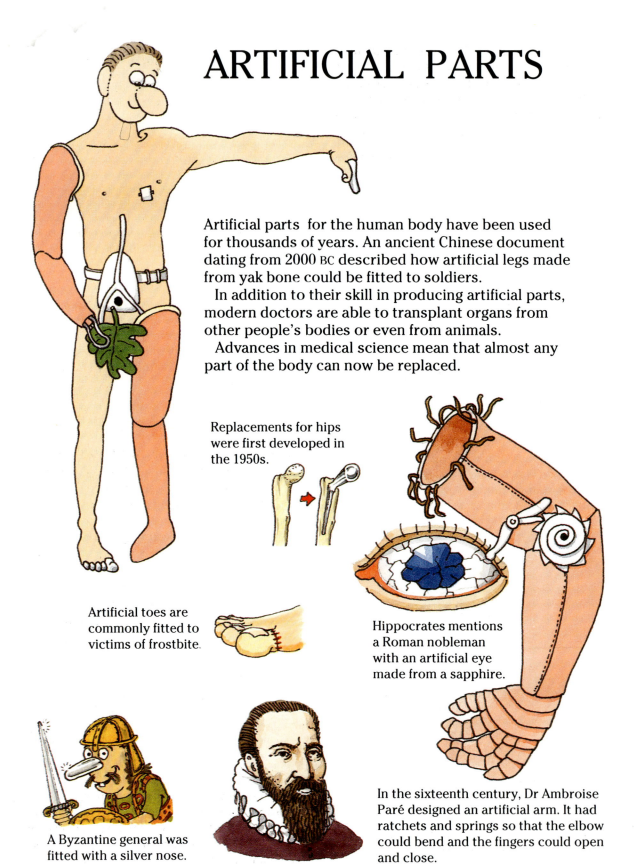

Artificial parts for the human body have been used for thousands of years. An ancient Chinese document dating from 2000 BC described how artificial legs made from yak bone could be fitted to soldiers.

In addition to their skill in producing artificial parts, modern doctors are able to transplant organs from other people's bodies or even from animals.

Advances in medical science mean that almost any part of the body can now be replaced.

Replacements for hips were first developed in the 1950s.

Artificial toes are commonly fitted to victims of frostbite.

Hippocrates mentions a Roman nobleman with an artificial eye made from a sapphire.

A Byzantine general was fitted with a silver nose.

In the sixteenth century, Dr Ambroise Paré designed an artificial arm. It had ratchets and springs so that the elbow could bend and the fingers could open and close.

Artificial pacemakers help the heart to beat regularly. The pacemaker is fitted under the skin and connected to the heart by electronic wires. Batteries are changed every two years. When someone dies, the pacemaker must be removed before cremation or it may explode.

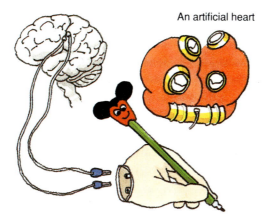

An artificial heart

Using biotechnology, artificial parts can be directly linked to the body nerves so that the artificial part can be operated by the brain.

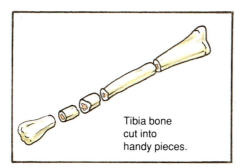

Tibia bone cut into handy pieces.

Bone banks store bone for use in operations. Bones are often cut into small chips for easy storing.

The first eye bank was started in New York in 1944. Eyes can only be stored for a short time before they become useless for surgery. Speed is essential.

In the eighteenth century some French scientists attempted to transplant the heart of a sheep.

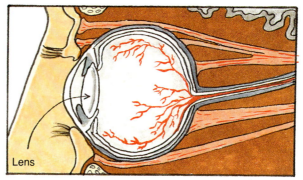

Cataracts are a clouding of the lens of the eye. The ancient Hindus were removing cataracts 4,000 years ago. Today the lens can be removed and replaced with a contact lens.

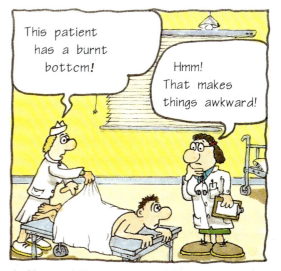

At Harvard University in 1984, two burn victims were given skin grafts. The skin had been grown in the laboratory 'skin farm' from tiny pieces. One square centimetre grew to half a square metre. Skin for transplants is often taken from the victim's bottom.

85

HOSPITALS

In the nineteenth century, operations such as leg amputations took place on the wards. The patients in the beds on either side tried to sleep through the terrifying screams and spurting blood.

Sick people coming into hospital bring infections with them. As many as ten per cent of patients receive an infection while they are in hospital.

Early purpose-built hospitals were dirty and overcrowded. The nurses were often drunk. For most of history, hospitals have been dangerous places to be in. This started to change at the end of the nineteenth century.

The word 'hospital' comes from the Latin word *hospitalis* meaning 'a place for guests'. The idea of a hospital as we understand it today dates from AD 331 when Constantine, the first Christian Roman Emperor, abolished earlier pagan treatment centres.

From the early days of Christianity, Christians were concerned with healing. Phoebe, a Roman noblewoman and friend of Saint Paul, turned her house into a hospital.

As early as 4000 BC there were Greek temples of healing in what is now Turkey. They were dedicated to gods such as Asclepius or Saturn.

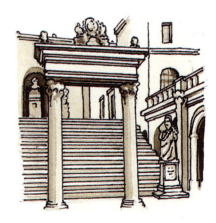

Entrance to Monte Casino, Europe's oldest monastic infirmary.

The oldest working hospital in the world is the Hôtel Dieu in Paris. It was founded in AD 600.

In the eighteenth century, the biggest cockroaches in England were said to be at St. Thomas' Hospital. They fed on blood and skin.

Florence Nightingale reformed the nursing profession in the nineteenth century. She insisted that nurses should be clean and wear uniforms. Her reforms began while she was treating British soldiers wounded in the Crimean War. Soon her influence spread round the world. In 1873, two nursing schools following Nightingale's principles were opened in New York.

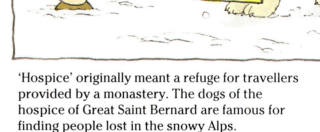

'Hospice' originally meant a refuge for travellers provided by a monastery. The dogs of the hospice of Great Saint Bernard are famous for finding people lost in the snowy Alps.

Originally, nuns, or sisters, used to tend to the sick. That's why senior nurses in hospitals are known as 'sisters' today.

The Arabs established major hospitals in Baghdad and Cordoba in the ninth century. At that time, Arabic medical knowledge was in advance of Europe.

OPEN WIDE!

Dentistry is the branch of medicine concerned with the teeth and gums. For many centuries, dentistry in Europe was carried out by barbers and barber surgeons, or by travelling healers.

Only in the sixteenth century did dentistry start to become a separate speciality. By 1622, dental surgery was a recognised profession in France.

Dentists were active in the USA by 1800. This was probably because the teeth of the colonists were considered the worst in the world. The founding of the first dental schools in the USA helped establish America as the world's leading centre of dental science.

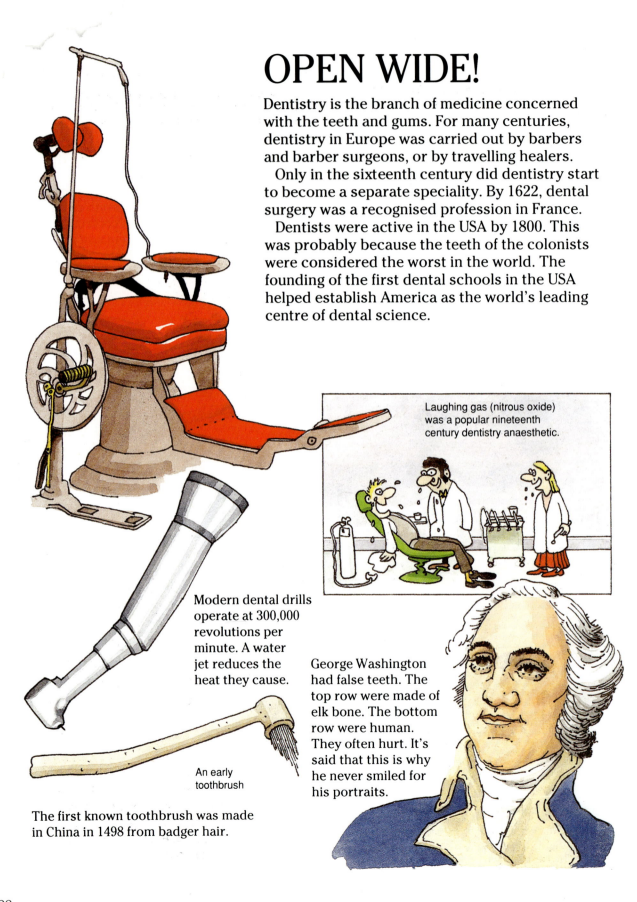

Laughing gas (nitrous oxide) was a popular nineteenth century dentistry anaesthetic.

Modern dental drills operate at 300,000 revolutions per minute. A water jet reduces the heat they cause.

An early toothbrush

The first known toothbrush was made in China in 1498 from badger hair.

George Washington had false teeth. The top row were made of elk bone. The bottom row were human. They often hurt. It's said that this is why he never smiled for his portraits.

Bad teeth and sweets

Sweet foods cause tooth decay. This was first observed by the ancient Greeks.

The Romans ate very little sugar. When the bodies of the victims of the eruption of Vesuvius were uncovered, they were found to have almost perfect teeth.

Elizabeth I of England had jet black teeth caused by tooth decay. Many Elizabethans had rotten teeth and bad breath. They loved marzipan.

Modern Western diet is rich in sugar. Twenty-nine million Americans over twenty years old have no natural teeth of their own. One third of all Americans over thirty-five need dentures.

From clay tablets dated around 3500 BC we know that the ancient Sumerians believed that toothache was caused by tiny worms which gnawed the teeth.

Ancient Etruscan dental bridge

False teeth have been used for thousands of years. Ivory, bone and even wood were used to make them.

Teeth from soldiers killed at the Battle of Waterloo were removed and made into false teeth for other people's mouths.

Scurvy caused by the lack of fresh vegetables or fruit was common among sailors. It causes teeth to fall out and gums to rot.

LOOKING AND FEELING GOOD

Ideas differ on what a healthy person should look like. For instance, in some cultures fatness is admired; in others it is despised. Fat women are admired in Africa and the Middle East. Among several African tribes young women eat special diets to fatten themselves up. Throughout history the people of many cultures have suffered extreme and often bizarre treatments in pursuit of beauty.

Mineral water has been considered healthy since the time of the Romans. In the eighteenth century, whole towns began to grow up around springs of mineral water. In the nineteenth century, long holidays in pure air became popular among the rich. Sanatoriums were built in mountains and other clean, cool, remote places to help treat tuberculosis. Today we have fitness centres and health farms.

The ancient Greeks loved physical beauty. There were physical education programmes in Greece by 700 BC. All Greek boys were taught to fight and run. But by AD 400 and until AD 1500 most sport was thought sinful in Europe.

From ancient times the Hindus have treated bathing, skin care, teeth cleaning and eye washes as religious necessities. It is said that some Hindu yogis can even pull out their intestines and clean them.

Native Americans along the coast of Oregon practised 'head flattening'. Babies' heads were tied to a cradle board so that the skull grew flat. Curiously, the Flathead tribe never did this.

In 1882, false eyelashes that had to be sewn on to the eyelids were advertised for sale in parts of the United States.

In Imperial China the feet of small girls were bound tightly so that the growth of their feet was restricted. This produced the tiny 'lily foot' which was thought attractive. Unfortunately, the girls were crippled for life.

Spas are towns which have grown up around a source of natural mineral water. They are called spas after the town of Spa in Belgium, which was a very popular source of mineral water. The town of Bath was the most fashionable of the English spas. In the nineteenth century at Bath people bathed in the waters fully clothed.

Bath
early nineteenth century

Some African and South American tribes will not allow young men to marry unless they have contracted malaria.

The Padaung women of Burma stretch their necks up to 40 cm long by wearing an increasing number of brass rings. The neck bones become dislocated and eventually the neck is too weak to support the head without the help of the rings.

In the Middle Ages, European children were thought to be unhealthy if they did not have any mild symptoms of eczema, a skin disease.

Cosmetic surgery

Rhytidectomy - standard facelift
The surgeon cuts the skin beyond the hairline, and pulls the facial skin tightly over the temples and towards the ears. The stretched skin is sewn into place and the excess skin is snipped off.

Liposuction
Liposuction is a technique for sucking fat from the neck, thighs and ankles. A blunt hollow tool called a probelike or a cannula is pushed into the fat through a small cut in the skin. It is attached to a mechanical suction machine and works like a vacuum cleaner.

Rib removal
The bottom rib can be removed to make the waist narrower.

PREVENTIVE MEDICINE

Preventive medicine means trying to stay healthy and not to get sick. This can be easier and cheaper than treating people after they have become sick. Preventive medicine involves health education and mass treatments such as vaccination for polio. It may also involve major public works such as new sewerage systems or fresh water supplies. Since Edward Jenner discovered the principle of vaccination in 1796, this has become the most successful of all preventive medicines. By 1980, the World Health Organisation had declared that their vaccination campaign had eradicated smallpox.

In the 1660s the boys of Eton School were punished if they did not smoke tobacco. It was thought that the smoke would protect them from the Great Plague. Today we know that tobacco smoke is not a preventive medicine; in fact it's very dangerous. Half of all long-term smokers die from diseases caused by smoking.

Some early preventive medicines

Eat carrots to prevent night blindness.

Wear a hat during a full moon to prevent madness.

Drink powdered eggshells in milk to prevent bedwetting.

In Britain, 'nit nurses' used to travel round schools. They inspected children's heads for small insects called nits.

In the Far East, many people wear a face mask if they have a cold. This is to stop them giving their germs to others.

The spread of diseases can sometimes be prevented if infected people are isolated. This is called quarantining. 'Quarantine' comes from an Italian word meaning forty. Ships suspected of carrying a disease had to wait forty days before being allowed to enter an Italian port. Travellers had to wait forty days outside medieval Italian towns before being allowed to enter.

Nowadays in the West there is so much food that many people eat too much of it. Too much salt can cause high blood pressure which can lead to heart attacks. Education about healthy eating helps people to live longer.

Campaigns to stop people smoking are an important part of modern health education. The following organs which had been damaged by smoking were removed in Australia in 1986:

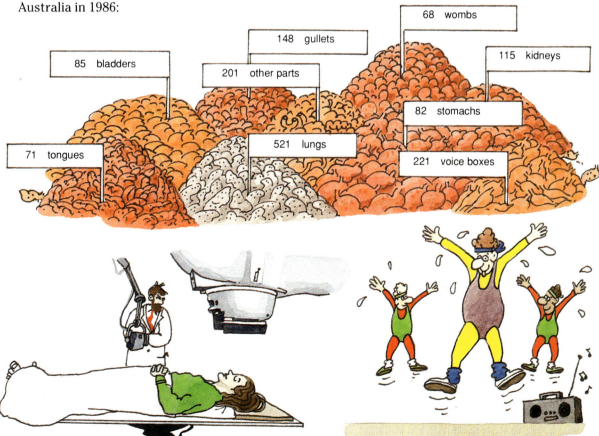

Many types of cancer can be cured, if they are detected early enough, by using small doses of nuclear radiation. Cancer screening programs ensure that people at risk visit a clinic regularly, even if they are feeling well.

Regular exercise prevents many illnesses. Nowadays, public education programmes encourage people to take exercise.

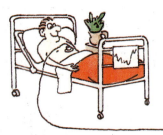

Visits to the doctor may become a thing of the past. Already heart monitors can transfer details of a beating heart down a telephone line to a hospital computer. Soon patients may be able to tell all their complaints to computers which will then decide on treatments and dispense medicines.

THE FUTURE

On average, people in the developed world live twice as long today as they did a hundred years ago. This is partly due to advancing medical techniques. Scientists are now trying to prevent the aging process.

Meanwhile, in the developing world, millions die young from diseases which are caused by poverty, ignorance and a lack of food and medicines.

Tiny bioelectronic devices can stimulate nerve cells. They enable the brain to operate artificial parts directly. Perhaps bioelectronics are the first step towards replacing the brain entirely.

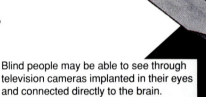

Blind people may be able to see through television cameras implanted in their eyes and connected directly to the brain.

People with speech defects may be able to speak through electronic voice boxes connected directly to the speech centres of the brain.

Mary had a pickled ham whose knees were nice as Joe...

Hickory Dickory Dock, the mouse ate Mr Spock...

Hmm! You need a bit of adjustment!

Every cell of the body contains DNA molecules. These molecules control who we are and how we grow. Scientists can alter DNA molecules by genetic engineering. In the future, it may be possible to create 'designer people' who will be physically perfect. But what will happen to the rest of us?

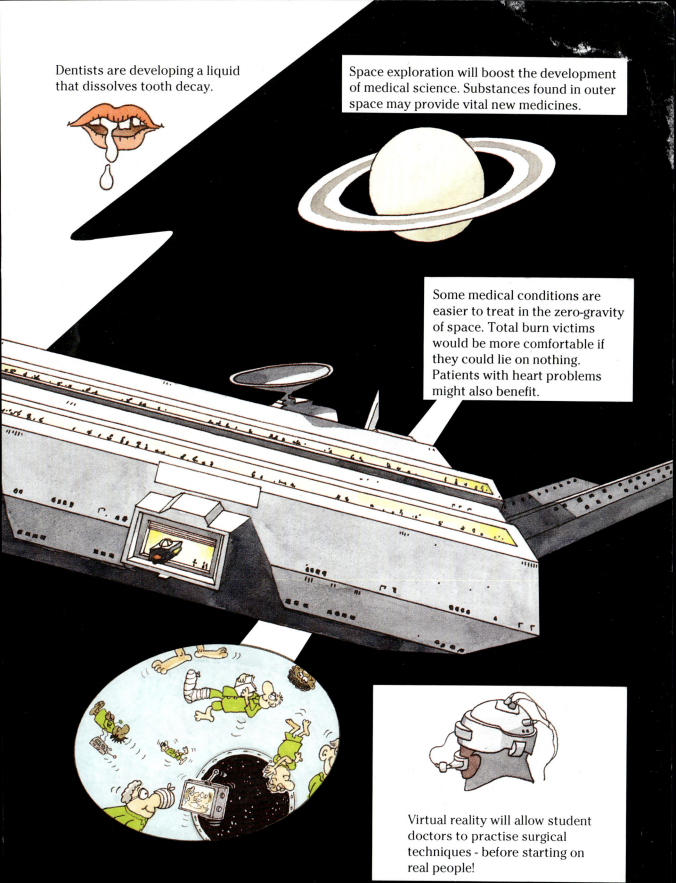

DEAD!

DYING

All living things die. It's the one thing we can all be certain of. In the past, dying was a lot more unpleasant than it is today. The average age of people when they died in the Stone Age was less than eighteen years. The main causes of death were disease and violence.

Fortunately, in western countries nowadays, most people die peacefully in old age. There are even special nursing homes called hospices to care for people who are dying of incurable illnesses.

On the island of Samoa sick old chiefs used to ask to be buried alive.

The image of the Grim Reaper is often associated with death.

Some species of mayfly live for only a few hours after they emerge from their larvae.

The lifespan of the elephant is roughly the same as that of humans - about seventy years.

Different cultures have different ways of dying. Old people of the Omaha tribe of Native Americans would stay behind when the rest of their family group moved camp. They were left enough food for just a few days.

Some species of birds live to a great age. Cocky, a male sulphur-crested cockatoo, died in London in 1982 aged over 80.

The most famous hospice in the world was founded by a nun called Mother Teresa. Her hospice was founded to look after people dying on the streets of Calcutta.

Buddhists believe that their dying thoughts will have an important influence on their next life.

Some Hindus try to say the word 'om' with their last breath. They believe that this may help them to escape the cycle of reincarnation.

Trees live a lot longer than animals. The oldest tree is thought to be 'General Sherman', a giant sequoia tree in California about 3,000 years old.

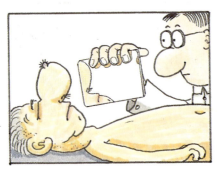

Test for death: Mirror
Breath should cause steam to appear on a mirror held to the mouth.

Test for death: Pulse
A pulse shows that the heart is still beating.

Test for death: Light
A modern test for brain stem death is to see if the pupils of the eye contract in bright light.

TESTING FOR DEATH

Death doesn't happen to all parts of a body at once. It takes time. For instance, brain cells die four minutes after the heart has stopped beating, but arterial grafts can be made seventy-two hours later. So it's not always easy to know exactly when somebody is dead.

The effects of extreme cold, called hypothermia, and of certain trance-like states such as catalepsy, have often been mistaken for death because breathing and heartbeat couldn't be detected. In fact, in the past, burial alive by mistake may have been quite common.

Nowadays, death is said to have happened when the brain stem stops working. The brain stem sits at the back of the skull. It controls vital body functions such as heartbeat and breathing. Modern instruments can detect breathing and heartbeat very accurately.

Queen Anne Boleyn's head continued to move its lips after it had been chopped off.

Around 1308 the philosopher Duns Scotus was buried in a vault in Cologne. When the vault was reopened shortly after, Duns Scotus was found outside his coffin. His hands were torn from trying to open the door of the vault. He had been buried alive.

Test for death: Blood
The Romans would chop off a finger to see if it bled.

Test for Death: Smoke
Some tribes of Native Americans would blow smoke up the bottom to test for any revival of life.

Test for Death: Nipple Forceps
In the nineteenth century Dr Josat invented a pair of nipple forceps to test for reaction to pain. Reaction to pain is also a modern test for brain stem death.

Many people stay up all night beside the body of a dead friend or relative. One reason for this custom is to make sure that the dead person is really dead and not just unconscious.

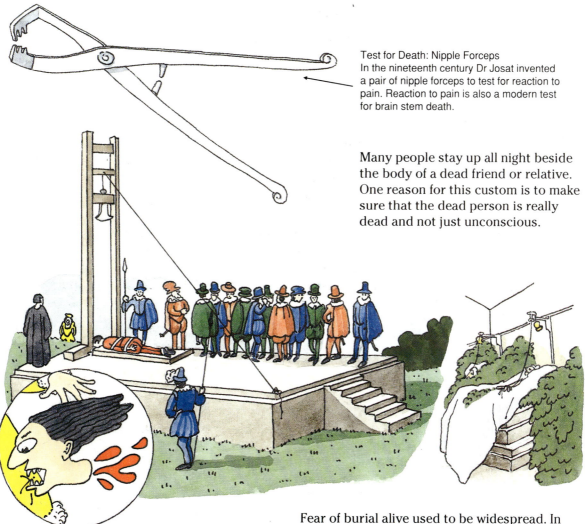

In 1541 the head of a woman guillotined on the Halifax gibbet flew through the air and gripped the clothing of a passerby with its teeth.

Fear of burial alive used to be widespread. In the Munich Waiting Mortuary, founded in 1791, corpses were kept for up to seventy-two hours in a sloping position before burial. Cords were attached to their fingers in such a way that the slightest movement would cause bells to ring.

101

DEAD BODIES

After death the muscles of the body relax. Relaxation starts in the jaw which falls open, and then spreads out through the body. At the same time, because the blood has stopped circulating, it sinks and causes stains on the skin which look like bruises. About six hours later, rigor mortis sets in. This is a stiffening of the muscles which again starts at the jaw and spreads out through the body. Rigor mortis normally lasts about thirty hours, then relaxation of the muscles spreads out once more from the jaw. Rigor mortis may set in immediately if death occurs at a time of stress. This is why suicides may be found gripping the revolver or sword with which they killed themselves.

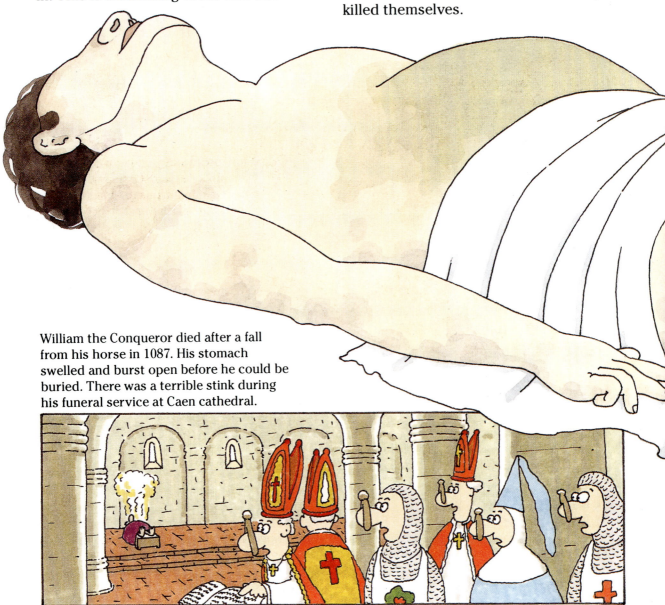

William the Conqueror died after a fall from his horse in 1087. His stomach swelled and burst open before he could be buried. There was a terrible stink during his funeral service at Caen cathedral.

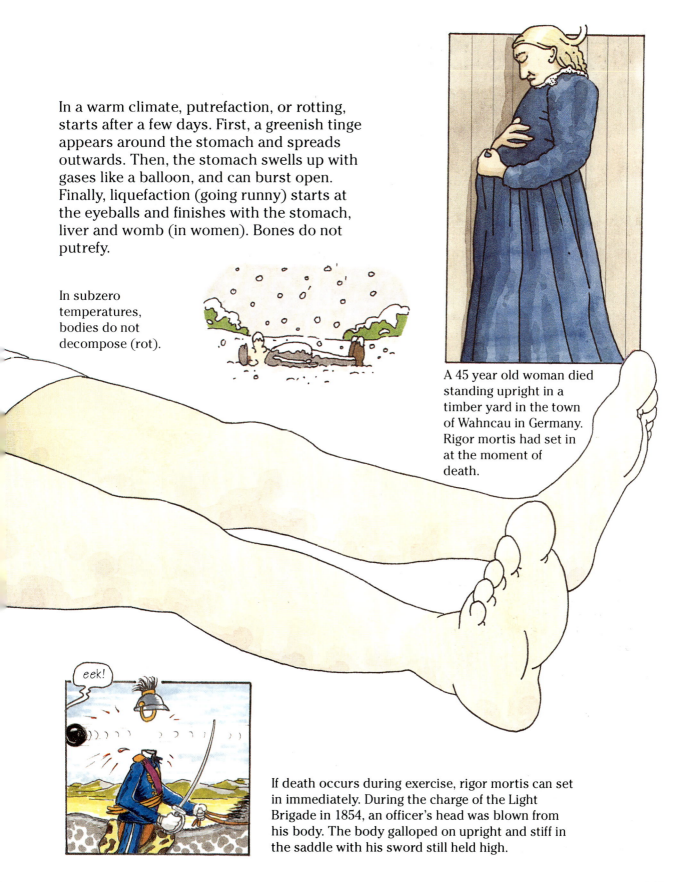

In a warm climate, putrefaction, or rotting, starts after a few days. First, a greenish tinge appears around the stomach and spreads outwards. Then, the stomach swells up with gases like a balloon, and can burst open. Finally, liquefaction (going runny) starts at the eyeballs and finishes with the stomach, liver and womb (in women). Bones do not putrefy.

In subzero temperatures, bodies do not decompose (rot).

A 45 year old woman died standing upright in a timber yard in the town of Wahncau in Germany. Rigor mortis had set in at the moment of death.

If death occurs during exercise, rigor mortis can set in immediately. During the charge of the Light Brigade in 1854, an officer's head was blown from his body. The body galloped on upright and stiff in the saddle with his sword still held high.

FUNERALS

About two million people die every year in the USA alone, so dealing with dead bodies is a major industry. Normally the first people to handle the dead are nurses and doctors. They tidy the hair and nails, tie up the jaw, put a plug in the bottom and probably they will remove dentures and jewellery. From that point the funeral directors, or undertakers, take over. They take the body away in a temporary coffin and prepare it for burial or cremation. The funeral director's job includes embalming the corpse, supplying the coffin, sending out invitations for the funeral and booking time at a crematorium or buying a plot of land for a burial. In the past, undertakers were often carpenters, because carpenters knew how to make coffins.

The coffin should be the height of the body plus two inches, and it should be the width of the shoulders across. Traditionally, coffins were made of oak or elm; nowadays, they are more likely to be made of veneered chipboard.

The death mask of Samuel Johnson

Death masks often are made by moulding clay around the face of a dead person. When the clay is removed there is a perfect impression of the dead person's face on the inside of it, and it can be used as a mould.

Coffin linings are made of base and side sheets which are attached to the coffin, a loose flap to cover the body and a face cloth to cover the head.

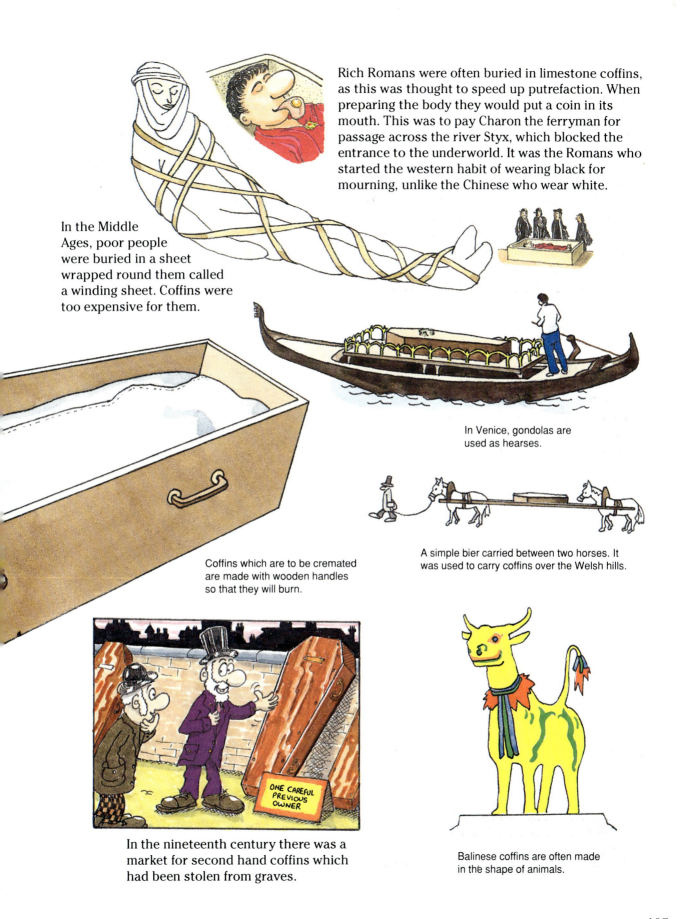

Rich Romans were often buried in limestone coffins, as this was thought to speed up putrefaction. When preparing the body they would put a coin in its mouth. This was to pay Charon the ferryman for passage across the river Styx, which blocked the entrance to the underworld. It was the Romans who started the western habit of wearing black for mourning, unlike the Chinese who wear white.

In the Middle Ages, poor people were buried in a sheet wrapped round them called a winding sheet. Coffins were too expensive for them.

In Venice, gondolas are used as hearses.

Coffins which are to be cremated are made with wooden handles so that they will burn.

A simple bier carried between two horses. It was used to carry coffins over the Welsh hills.

In the nineteenth century there was a market for second hand coffins which had been stolen from graves.

Balinese coffins are often made in the shape of animals.

Home guide to head shrinking

Remove the head from the body.

Make a cut from the back of the neck to the crown of the head.

Remove the skin from the skull and discard the skull.

Sew the eyelids together. Sew the lips together.

EMBALMING

Nowadays many bodies are embalmed. It makes them look peaceful and it stops them smelling before the funeral.

The body is first placed on a trolley and washed in soap and water. Then embalming fluid is pumped into it through an opening in a vein, normally near the armpit. Embalming fluid is a mixture of preservative (usually formaldehyde), disinfectant and colouring. As the fluid spreads through the veins, the body regains a healthy pink colour. Then, after four to six pints have been pumped in, the blood is drained out of the body through another opened vein into a vacuum container on the floor.

The process of replacing the blood with embalming fluid takes about three-quarters of an hour. Afterwards, a surgical instrument called a trocar is plunged into the abdomen and scooped around until all the soft tissue has been removed. Cavity fluid is then pumped in to fill up the empty space.

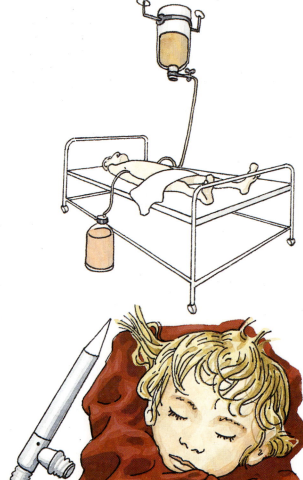

In order to give the face a calm expression, the jaw is sewn tight with thread through the inside of the lips. This is a picture of Rosalia Lombardo of Palermo, Sicily, who died in 1920 aged two. Rosalia's face is especially peaceful and well-preserved by injections given to her body immediately after death.

Boil the scalp and face for two hours.

Place hot stones in the scalp to shrink the skin.

Smoke overnight.

Hang above the fireplace.

Bodies are sometimes embalmed naturally. Tollund Man, who was probably a fertility sacrifice to the goddess Ertha around 500 BC, was preserved intact in a peat bog until discovered in 1950 at Tollund in Denmark. His features are so well-preserved that even the stubble of his beard is completely visible.

Tourists queue to see Lenin's body in his open tomb outside the walls of the Kremlin, Moscow.

A preserved head from ancient Peru. A cactus spine has been inserted through the lips.

Perhaps the most famous body to be embalmed this century is that of Lenin, the leader of the Russian revolution. The body is kept in a temperature-controlled mausoleum in Red Square, Moscow, and is visited by thousands of tourists every year. Every eighteen months the body is taken out and soaked in a special preservative fluid.

In ancient Babylon, bodies were sometimes embalmed in honey. It is said that the body of Alexander the Great was preserved like this.

The Egyptians had several different beliefs about the after-life. Here is one of them:

Ba, the soul, could enter or leave the body at will. It was pictured as a human-headed bird.

After death, Ba made a dangerous journey to the Kingdom of Osiris. A ferryman with eyes in the back of his head took Ba across a river.

Osiris judged new souls at midnight. Ba was then weighed against the feather of virtue. If he had been good, the feather would be heavier.

MUMMIES AND EMBALMING

The ancient Egyptians believed that it was necessary to preserve the body of a dead person in order for that dead person to be reborn. Belief in resurrection after death was centred around the cult of the god Osiris. Osiris was born a man, died, and was mummified by the heavenly doctor Anubis; he was then reborn as a god. The Egyptians believed that by following the same process of mummification, they too could be resurrected. Millions of Egyptians were mummified during the course of the ancient Egyptian civilisation.

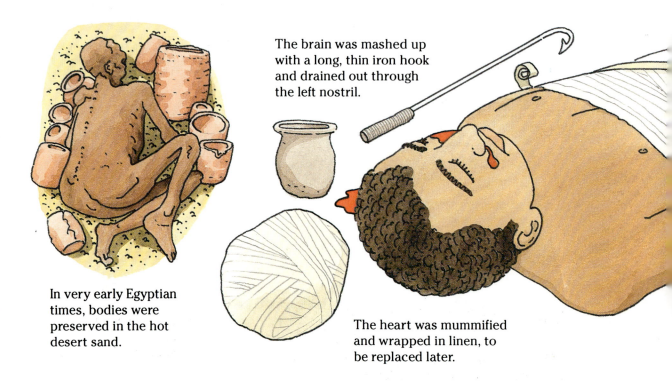

In very early Egyptian times, bodies were preserved in the hot desert sand.

The brain was mashed up with a long, thin iron hook and drained out through the left nostril.

The heart was mummified and wrapped in linen, to be replaced later.

Good souls were given land in the kingdom of Osiris.

Bad souls were roasted in a fire and hacked to pieces.

Anubis was the god of the dead. He had the head of a jackal.

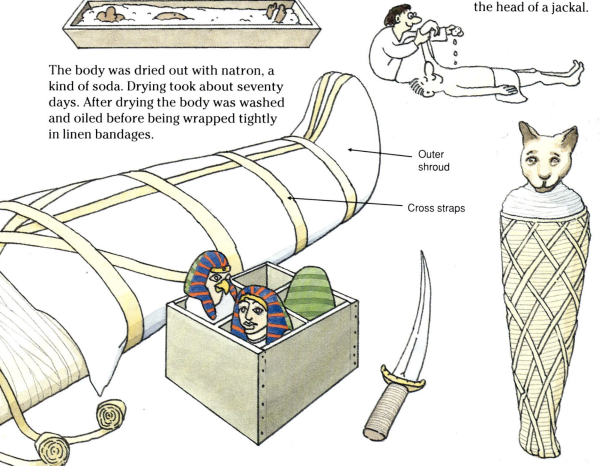

The body was dried out with natron, a kind of soda. Drying took about seventy days. After drying the body was washed and oiled before being wrapped tightly in linen bandages.

Outer shroud

Cross straps

Intestines and other organs were removed through a cut in the abdomen. The priest would plunge his arm in up to the armpit to reach to the top of the lungs. Internal organs were often kept separately in special pots called canopic jars.

Mummified cats were sacred to Bast, the goddess of pleasure.

BURIAL

If dead bodies are left lying around, they quickly rot and become a danger to health. Throughout history the commonest way to dispose of the dead has been to bury them underground. In some of the earliest graves of prehistoric Europe, stones were often laid on top of a body. It was thought that this would stop the dead from returning to haunt the living. For the same reason the feet were often tied together. Red ochre might be sprinkled on a body to represent the blood and strength it would need in an afterlife.

In modern graves there should be a depth of about six feet between the coffin lid and the surface. At the end of the funeral a few handfuls of earth are scattered on the coffin. The rest of the earth is replaced using a mechanical digger after the mourners have left.

The Vikings sometimes buried their dead under the thresholds of their houses. This was because they thought that the souls of the dead could defend their houses against evil spirits.

If a body is to be buried at sea, holes must be drilled into the coffin so that water can get in to make the coffin sink.

Other ways to dispose of bodies

The Aborigines of Australia left dead bodies in trees.

Hurry up – He's going off!

In the Solomon Islands the dead were laid out on a reef for the sharks to eat.

Tibetans have no respect for dead bodies once the soul has left them, and will even hack them to pieces for the birds to eat.

In China it is considered very important to bury a corpse in the right spot. An astrological chart with an inset compass is often used to determine the exact position and alignment for the body.

Suicide is a sin in the Christian religion. People who committed suicide were not allowed burial in Christian graveyards and were often buried at crossroads.

Fear of burial alive was widespread in the nineteenth century. A special apparatus was invented by Count Karnice-Karnicki which involved a vertical tube running from the coffin to a box above ground level. A glass sphere resting on the chest of the corpse was connected via the tube to a flag, a light and a loud bell. Any small movement of the chest would activate the mechanism.

High in the mountains of the Hindu Kush, bodies are buried upright in the snow.

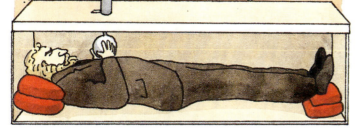

Muslims like to be buried on the same day as they die. The body should be placed on its right side, facing Mecca. On the other hand, Buddhists like to be buried facing north.

Some Inuits cover the corpse with a small igloo. Because of the cold the body will remain for ever unless it is eaten by polar bears.

The Parsees of Bombay used to leave their dead on the top of tall towers to be eaten by vultures. The vultures devour the corpses to the bone within five minutes.

GRAVEYARDS

Cemeteries are places for burial other than churchyards. Cemetery comes from the Greek word *koimeterion* which means 'dormitory'.

Christians were originally buried inside churches, not below ground.

By AD 752, many churches had become ridiculously overcrowded with dead bodies. Arms and legs sometimes stuck out of the floors and walls. So a decree from the Pope allowed graveyards to be added to churches.

However, by the seventeenth century, the same problem of overcrowding was ruining the graveyards. Between 1810 and 1830 in one graveyard in London 14,000 bodies were buried, some only two feet deep. Bones were even dug up and sold to make fertiliser.

By the nineteenth century, the case for cemeteries separate from churchyards became overwhelming. One of the first major cemeteries to be built was the Père Lachaise in Paris.

Forest Lawns Memorial Parks near Los Angeles, America, comprises four cemeteries which cover an area of two square miles. The first, established at Glendale in 1914, is home to the largest religious painting in the USA.

Emperor Constantine

The ancient Greeks and Romans used to bury their dead outside their cities. But during the Roman Empire the fashion grew for burial in underground chambers, called catacombs, within the city of Rome.

Early Christians dug catacombs beneath the church of St. Peter, the first Pope, so that they could be buried near to Peter's body. From there it was a small step to burial inside the church. The first person to be buried inside a church was the Emperor Constantine in AD 337.

In the nineteenth century, Mr Wilson of London planned to build a pyramid which would have been bigger than that of Cheops, big enough to house five million bodies. Wilson's pyramid would have been the largest cemetery ever built, but it was never completed.

As churches became more crowded, bodies were sometimes removed from graves and placed in charnel houses.

There are thousands of bones in the charnel house of the Capuchin Church of the Immaculate Conception in Rome, arranged in complicated designs on the ceilings and walls.

To increase the popularity of the Père Lachaise cemetery, its owners dug up the bodies of famous people and reburied them there. Among the famous people reburied in this way were the playwrights Molière and Beaumarchais.

At the charnel house of the Capuchin Monastery in Palermo, Sicily, the bodies were first dried and are preserved fully clothed.

The Brookwood cemetery near Woking in Southern England was opened in 1854. A special railway, called the Brookwood Necropolis Railway, was built to carry coffins from London, sixty miles away.

The Taj Mahal is one of the seven wonders of the modern world. It was built by the Mogul Emperor Shah-Jehan for his favourite wife Arjamund Begum. Arjamund died in 1631. Work on the mausoleum started in 1632.

MEMORIALS

The earliest Christian tombstones were simple stone slabs known as ledgers. Later the ledgers were sometimes raised up on legs to form table tombs. Chest tombs were table tombs with the sides enclosed.

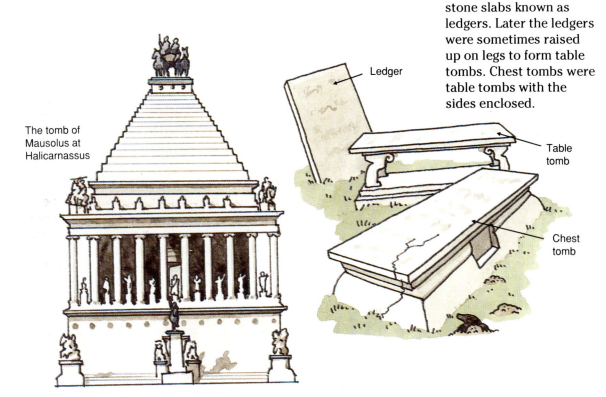

The tomb of Mausolus at Halicarnassus

It is human vanity to hope that we shall be remembered after we die. In many historic cultures, more money has been spent on memorials for the dead than on homes for the living. The richer and more powerful the dead person, the bigger the memorial. Mausolus was a Persian King in what is now south-western Turkey. His huge, white marble tomb at Halicarnassus was one of the Seven Wonders of the Ancient World. It was built by his wife Artemisia (who was also his sister). Artemisia mixed his ashes in wine and drank the mixture. She later joined him in their mausoleum.

It took 20,000 men working for 22 years to build the Taj Mahal.

The Emperor wanted his building to be unique. When it was finished, the hands of the craftsmen were chopped off so that they couldn't build another one like it.

Elvis Presley is buried at his home called Gracelands, in Memphis, USA, which is now an Elvis museum as well as his mausoleum.

The burial mounds of native North American Indians were sometimes built in the shapes of birds and animals. Some of these mounds were built as early as 700 BC.

Great Serpent Mound, Ohio

The tomb built for the Chinese Emperor Qin Shihuangdi was said to contain rivers of mercury. Crossbows were set to fire at grave robbers automatically. The workmen who built the tomb were walled up inside to stop them giving away the secrets of its construction.

The great pyramids are among the largest structures ever built. The pyramid of Cheops is made up of 2,500,000 blocks of stone of an average weight of 2.5 tonnes. Its height is over 140 metres and 100,000 workers took more than 20 years to build it.

The tomb of Karl Marx, the founder of communism, is in Highgate Cemetery in London.

GRAVE ROBBERS

Nowadays, to help science, many people give their bodies for medical research. Enough bodies are given each year for the researchers and medical students who need them. It wasn't always so easy. For many years, Christians believed that at the end of the world their physical bodies would be resurrected. If bodies were cut up by researchers, resurrection would be impossible.

Post-mortems were carried out by Christians in Byzantium as early as AD 50. In Parma in 1286, bodies were cut open to try to discover the cause of the plague. These were exceptions. Even as late as 1380, Pope Boniface banned the boiling or cutting up of corpses. It was only during the Renaissance that dissection was permitted in Europe. Even then, it was only allowed on the bodies of executed criminals.

There was always a shortage of bodies. And the shortage grew worse with the growth of medical schools in the eighteenth century. Medical students needed bodies to practise on. Grave robbers, or resurrectionists, stepped in to supply the bodies.

Grave robbing made easy

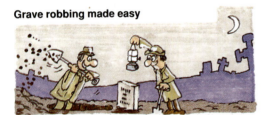

Dig a vertical shaft to the head of the coffin.

Cover with sacking to reduce the noise.

Prise off the coffin lid.

Haul out the body using a noose tied round the neck.

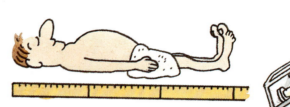

Children's bodies were often sold by the foot: six shillings for the first foot and nine pence per inch thereafter.

The Crouch gang was one of the most famous gangs of grave robbers. They operated in London in the early 1800s.

This picture is taken from *The Resurrectionists* by the cartoonist Thomas Rowlandson (1756-1827).

William Harvey, who discovered that blood circulates round the body, dissected the dead bodies of his own father and sister.

In the sixteenth century, the French government gave one criminal per year to the medical profession for live dissection. Live dissection was also practised by Greek doctors in ancient Alexandria.

Mr Stapleton apparently died of typhus in 1831. His body was stolen by grave robbers. On the dissecting table, an electric wire was inserted into a cut in his chest. He sat up and said, 'I am alive.'

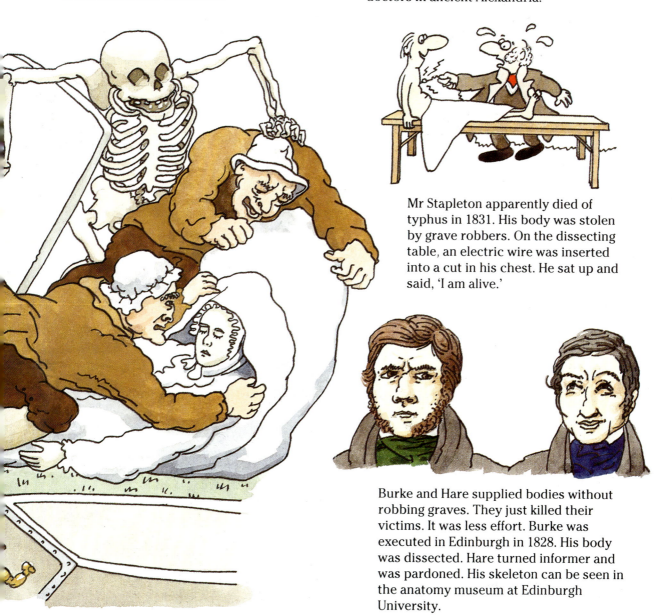

Burke and Hare supplied bodies without robbing graves. They just killed their victims. It was less effort. Burke was executed in Edinburgh in 1828. His body was dissected. Hare turned informer and was pardoned. His skeleton can be seen in the anatomy museum at Edinburgh University.

GRAVE GOODS

The custom of burying things with the dead is at least 60,000 years old. The rich and powerful were buried with treasure, and even with their servants. Ordinary people were buried with food and drink and sometimes cups and tools. Things may have been buried with dead bodies because it was believed that they would be useful in the after-life. Much of what we know about ancient people has been learned from studying their grave goods.

The tomb of the Qin Emperor of China contained an army of life-sized clay soldiers and the bodies of all his concubines who were killed specially for his burial.

Some Bronze Age people only buried a dead person's skull with a few possessions.

The Egyptian pyramids were like palaces stuffed with treasures. The tomb of Tutankhamun contained the largest hoard of ancient golden artefacts ever found.

In ancient China, jaw bones of pigs were buried with the dead.

Neanderthal graves 60,000 years old have been found containing the remains of flowers.

The Egyptian queen Her-Neith was buried with her favourite dog.

A thirteenth century Maharajah of Jaipur was buried with his favourite elephant.

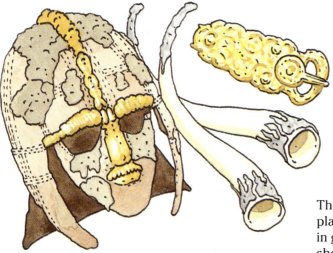

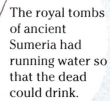
In India, a Mogul prince was buried with his barber.

The burial ship of a Saxon king dating from AD 650 was found at Sutton Hoo. It contained some of the richest treasures ever found in England.

In the Middle Ages, consecrated bread was buried in the grave, so that the dead could offer it to God. Priests were buried with a cross and a cup as well as the bread.

The Adena tribe of Ohio placed clay tobacco pipes in graves, in case the dead should wish to smoke.

The royal tombs of ancient Sumeria had running water so that the dead could drink.

Nowadays, if children die, their favourite toys may be buried with them.

Among other things, the ancient Celts would put games in the grave so that the dead would have something to amuse themselves with in the next world.

119

RELICS

The remains of bodies often have been thought to have magical powers.
The cannibals of Melanesia used to eat the bodies of their enemies, not for the meat, but in order to aquire the strength of their victims. They said the meat tasted of pork. They called the flesh of missionaries 'long pig'.

The bones of Christian saints are still thought by many to have miraculous powers, and pilgrims travel long distances to see them. Arm, leg and head bones are considered the most holy. In the Middle Ages, these holy relics were big business. Pilgrims had money to spend, just like tourists today. Bones were often divided up. John the Baptist's went to Amiens, Rhodes, Besançon and several other places. Today such beliefs are less common.

St Hugh of Lincoln bit off two pieces of Mary Magdelene's arm bone when on a pilgrimage to Normandy, and smuggled them back to England.

A Buddhist ritual trumpet made from a human thigh bone.

Food facts

Not only the Melanesians ate human flesh. Some aboriginal Australian tribes ate the flesh of dead relatives as a mark of respect.

In some parts of Indonesia the liquids of a decomposing body were mixed with rice and eaten. It was believed that this food had magical properties.

On some islands of Melanesia the skull of the deceased is given to a near relative to use as a drinking cup.

One of the vertebrae of the astronomer Galileo was stolen in 1757. It is now displayed in Padua.

One of the holiest shrines of Buddhism is the Temple of the Tooth at Kandy in Sri Lanka, where Buddha's left canine tooth is kept.

The ancient Celts hung the heads of their enemies from their horses and outside their houses.

A hair from the beard of the Prophet Mohammed is preserved in resin in the Topkapi museum in Istanbul.

Frederich Ruysh (1638-1731) made tableaux from the skeletons of children together with preserved parts of the human body and stuffed birds. His collection was bought by Peter the Great of Russia.

CREMATION

In AD 789, Emperor Charlemagne decreed death for anyone practising cremation. Cremation was considered unchristian because it was thought that a burned body could not be resurrected at the Last Judgement.

The first cremations in the USA were carried out in Washington in 1876, in the private crematorium of a doctor, Julius Lemogne. In Britain, the first legal cremation took place in 1883 when Dr William Price, an 83 year old Welsh druidic priest, cremated his five month old baby, whom he had named Jesus Christ Price.

Modern crematoriums reduce a body to ashes in about one and a half hours. The newest models working at temperatures up to 1,200 degrees centigrade are even quicker. Wood ash from the coffin is light, and goes up the chimney together with any water vapour, leaving the bones and the ashes of the body behind. Any metal, for instance gold from teeth, is collected from the ashes. Finally, the bone fragments are crushed to a fine powder in a special machine. The final residue per adult weighs about three kilograms. This is collected into a tin can with a screw top, ready to be emptied into an urn or to be scattered.

An early crematorium

The Beaker people who lived in Europe around 4,000 years ago used to collect the ashes of their dead in beakers or decorated pots.

Suttee was a cruel tradition common in India until banned by the British in 1829. Widows were expected to burn alive with their dead husbands, sometimes cradling their husband's head on their laps and lighting the fire themselves. In 1780, when Rajah Ajit Singh was cremated, sixty-four of his wives were burned alive with him.

Gypsy kings and queens are burned in their caravans.

Os resectum is a mixture of burial and cremation. A finger is cut off and buried, while the rest of the body is burned. The buried finger is the seed for the new body which will be resurrected on judgement day.

Viking leaders were placed in their favourite long boat, which was then set alight and pushed out to sea.

The poet Percy Bysshe Shelley drowned off the coast of Italy in 1822. His body was burned on an open fire on the beach. Wine, incense and oil were thrown on to the flames. Trelawney, his friend, plucked the heart from the fire, badly burning his own hand. The heart was returned to England in a box.

Nowadays, cremation is forbidden for orthodox Jews, Parsees, Muslims and Greek Orthodox Christians. Hindus always cremate their dead. The eldest son lights the funeral pyre.

123

LIFE AFTER DEATH

Most people throughout history have believed that their spirit continues to live after their mortal body is dead, although there has always been a minority of atheists who do not believe in God and think that when you're dead you're dead.

The ancient Mesopotamians believed that the souls of the dead fell into a huge pit called the 'Land of No Return'.

The Vikings believed that the souls of warriors who died in battle went to a life of feasting in Valhalla, the hall of the god Odin.

The ancient Celts believed that the afterworld was a place of happiness where they could indulge in all their favourite activities. There would be lots to eat and drink and plenty of fighting, and wounds would heal overnight. For this reason the Celts did not fear death and often went into battle naked.

Christians believe that the good go to Heaven and the bad go to Hell. However, there may be a long time to wait until Judgement Day. Because Hell is such a severe punishment, most Christians believe that the dead go to be purified before being admitted to heaven. This stage of purification is called purgatory and can be thought of as a temporary hell.

Pythagoras, the ancient Greek philosopher, believed that broad beans contained the souls of the dead so he forbade his followers to eat them.

Hindus and Buddhists believe that the soul experiences many lives. After death the soul is reborn in a new young body which can be an animal or a person. This is called reincarnation. Eventually very good, wise people can escape the cycle of reincarnation and enter into a state of one-ness with the universe called nirvana.

The Aborigines believe that their spirits exist before and after life in a state called Dreamtime. The spirits of the tribe and of its special animals are reborn again and again.

Muslims believe that the souls of warriors who die in a Jihad, or holy war, will go straight to heaven.

The Greek underworld was a grey place of shadows called the Kingdom of Hades. Dead people were pale shadows of their former selves. Hades was guarded by a giant three-headed dog called Cerberus and surrounded by the river Styx. A corner of Hades called Elysium was slightly more pleasant and was reserved for heroes.

Cryonics is a method of freeze drying bodies in the hope that they can be thawed out and brought back to life in the future. People ask for this treatment because they believe that a cure for the cause of their death may be discovered in the future.

After death the body must be connected immediately to a heart-lung machine and packed in water ice.

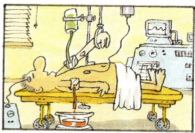

Later the blood is drained out of the body, and replaced with preservative fluid.

DEEP FROZEN FUTURE

The population of the world is now 5,000 million people and it's still growing. About 5 million tonnes of dead bodies have to be disposed of every year. The problems of disposal are going to increase in the future.

Cryonics poses many problems. In particular, would future generations want to revive thousands of frozen bodies?

Millions of bodies were mummified in ancient Egypt. If it were possible for us to revive them, would we want all those ancient Egyptians to look after?

In the USA today some people pay up to $150,000 to be mummified after death using techniques based on those of the ancient Egyptians.

Finally the body is frozen in liquid nitrogen. Keeping it frozen is very expensive.

It's unlikely that cryonics is effective. To really work, bodies should be frozen before they die.

The first dead body to be permanently frozen was James Bedford, a Californian teacher of psychology, in 1967.

Quick drying may be used in future to preserve bodies for later revival. In 1954 the body of a ten year old Inca prince was discovered in a cave on a mountain near Santiago, Chile. The child had died 500 years before but the body had been very well preserved in the cold, dry air.

The frozen bodies of mammoths have been found in the ice of Siberia. Their meat could still be eaten after thousands of years. In the future people may consider it wasteful to burn or bury 5 million tonnes of nutritious dead bodies every year. They could be frozen and eaten instead!

INDEX

Guilty!	**2-31**
Disaster!	**33-63**
Sick!	**65-95**
Dead!	**97-127**

First published in 1993 by Franklin Watts

This edition published in 1998

Franklin Watts
96 Leonard Street
London EC2A 4RH

Franklin Watts Australia
14 Mars Road
Lane Cove NSW 2006

© 1993 Lazy Summer Books Ltd
Illustrated by Lazy Summer Books Ltd

ISBN 0 7496 3120 1
A CIP catalogue record for this book is available from the British Library

Printed in Belgium